Additional Praise for *At Home in the New World*

Maria Terrone points her writing directly at the difficult and powerful material of the edges of ordinary life: a small hospitalized child being threatened by a nurse, horror stories from Vietnam, stories of a POW in a Japanese camp. But much more than that. Why does a beloved brother have a love affair with guns and shooting? What does it mean to explore our own fears unflinchingly? Her writing penetrates the underworld from the subway to the unconscious, from family to beyond, sometimes employing wry humor to examine her personal obsessions and her place in the "new world" of 21st century America. You will sink into these essays and be rapt with attention. A fine book.

—Joanna Clapps Herman, author of *The Anarchist Bastard* and the forthcoming *When I am Italian: Quando sono italiana*

The essays in Maria Terrone's *At Home in the New World* are a testament to the power of attention and curiosity. Like a generous host, Terrone tours us through her vast intellectual, emotional, and creative concerns with precision and personality. She finds the extraordinary in the ordinary, a reminder to readers to wake up to the world around us. This is a remarkable collection—charming, smart, and compulsively readable. A gift.

—Jessica Hendry Nelson, author of *If Only You People Could Follow Directions*

D1468734

VIA Folios 132

At Home
in the New World

At Home
in the New World

Maria Terrone

BORDIGHERA PRESS

Library of Congress Control Number: 2018947175

Printed in the United States.

Published by
BORDIGHERA PRESS
John D. Calandra Italian American Institute
25 West 43rd Street, 17th Floor
New York, NY 10036

VIA FOLIOS 132
ISBN 978-1-59954-127-3

CONTENTS

I. HIDE AND SEEK

MYSTERY, MENACE AND EARLY SORROW

The dolls never slept. They stayed wide eyed and unblinking on their shelf in my small, overheated room, watching me watch the man and woman in the apartment across the way. As a child with insomnia, I was wide eyed, too, although I would have preferred sleep. Strangely, the couple never appeared in the window frame together. The white satin slip the slim woman wore as she criss-crossed the room left a kind of afterglow as the robed man replaced her in the frame, a lit, otherworldly image that kept me awake even longer. I wondered about the lives of these adults who were nothing like the grown-ups I knew, realizing at the same time that I'd never know anything about them.

The regiment of dolls, lined up at attention in neat rows, functioned as my personal sentry. I felt most reassured by the ranks of the exotically dressed foreign-born who'd been brought to me by traveling friends and relatives. I suspected that they possessed secret military skills they wouldn't hesitate to use if the need arose, especially the bearded, dashing one from Saudi Arabia whom my brother and I named Abdullah. With a big leather water pouch slung over his shoulder and vigilant, piercing eyes, he was confident, ready for anything that might happen during the night. Relieved, I'd eventually allow sleep to claim me.

*

The child in the hospital bed across from mine was crying incon-solably in the darkness.

On the floor I could make out a rough-looking, shapeless bear. "SOMEONE PICK IT UP! PLEASE!" he wailed over and over.

I strained to hear footsteps. Nothing. Shouldn't a nurse come? Where could she be? At nine years old, having fallen off a low fence, bashing my skull on concrete on a visit to my grandmother, I was sleeping in a hospital for the first time in my life. The concussion diagnosis was minor compared to that other trauma, and I fought the terror by telling myself that this strange, sterile place had to be governed by the same rules and expectations as in the adult world I'd experienced so far.

But no one came, and the child, perhaps five years old, became more insistent. "SOMEONE! PLEASE! PICK UP TEDDY," he implored in panic and despair.

After what felt like forever, a nurse appeared. I sighed with relief as the woman in white bent over the low bars of the bed, her face very close to the boy's, in a gesture that brought to mind a wingless angel or, at least, a comforting mother figure.

"Shut up!" she snarled.

Her voice was deep—an animal's growl. In those two words, my world crashed. A seismic shift occurred, shaking my faith, upending everything I'd believed to be true. Only my physical, hairline fracture would heal completely.

I burrowed into my bed and pulled the sheet over my face, leaving only my eyes visible—and even then, I felt the need to hide completely, to erase myself. I played dead, a mute witness in the night, holding my breath, stilling my limbs, while straining to hear what would happen next. The child kept repeating his anguished plea, but this time the nurse answered, "Shut up, I said, or I'll give you the needle." I felt a sharp pain. I could not escape this blow, this knife thrust, this darkening of my once-bright heart.

*

In the Max Ernst painting, *Two Children Are Threatened by a Nightingale*, a girl/woman with wildly flying black hair holds out a small knife. Another lies on the ground as if she's fainted. Or maybe she's dead—her dress has the look of a bandage or mummy wrapping. A faceless man carrying a bundled child seems to be running atop a red wooden structure. Far off in the sky are the two curved paint strokes universally understood to represent a bird.

I first came upon this disquieting work in the Museum of Modern Art while researching surrealism for an independent high school project. Ernst said that it was inspired during a fevered hallucination of early childhood memories and dreams, which didn't surprise me. I was completely mesmerized as if in a dream, pulled in shuddering but held by a fascination that kept me rooted, unable to move on to another painting.

And yet, despite the work's title, I could find nothing threatening about the nightingale, so small and distant it seems an afterthought. Some critics believe the female is "brandishing" the knife, presumably for protection, as she faces in the bird's direction. In the scenario that I imagined, it's the adults who pose the threat. The woman with the knife possibly just murdered the woman lying near her feet, who could be the mother of the kidnapped infant being carried off by the man on the rooftop. The bird is innocent, a remote observer of human evil. Of course, I couldn't be sure, knowing only that this artwork communicated both mystery and menace.

*

It's summertime and nearly dusk. My husband and I are relaxing in a rented country house. We hear low voices and footsteps. At the window I see on the road a family of five, all blonde, all wearing the tasteful pastel cotton outfits that could fill the pages of a Lands End catalog. They move slowly as if under water, their flip flops smacking the tar rhythmically like water slapping itself. A blue astral light blinks in the ear of the teenage boy. When they murmur, their perfect incisors gleam, biting through the dark like the moon's mouth above their shoulders. I suddenly think of *The Invasion of the Body Snatchers*, that sci-fi film of deceptively normal-looking people who've actually been taken over by aliens. They go about their daily routine, hiding their nefarious plans.

Walking on the beach earlier that day, I'd seen two men in the far distance who appeared to be dressed in white from their legs up to their necks. Oddly, the words "sun protection" didn't enter my mind but "hazmat suits." But maybe they were a mirage, not intimations of disaster.

*

The volume of *Grimms' Fairy Tales* that I'd checked out of the library when I was eight filled me with horror by day and violent images by night. I still recoil recalling the scene of Cinderella's stepsisters chopping off their own toes and heels to fit into the golden (not glass) slipper. Evil characters were tortured in gruesome ways such as being thrown naked into a barrel of nails and having their eyes pecked out. But the most gruesome fates seemed to be reserved for the children—in one tale, a stepson is decapitated and cut up for stew that's so tasty, his father asks for a second helping. Even the black line drawings in the book had the sinister quality of a dark, tangled wood where children could easily be lost and ensnared. After reading several of the stories, which filled me with dread, I could read no more. "They're just fairy tales," I assured myself. "Nothing like this happens in real life."

I'd seen a few older kids in the schoolyard verbally attack and even push around the smaller children, but if one of the nuns witnessed such behavior, she would swiftly intervene with great wrath. In my world view, that's what grown-ups were there to do: protect the innocent and vulnerable. If the newspapers of the time reported horrendous stories of child abuse, as they do so often today, I was blissfully unaware.

*

During freshman year of college, I read Thomas Mann's "Disorder and Early Sorrow." That 1925 short story set in Germany left a strong impression on me that persisted over the years although I'd forgotten the plot and most of the characters. All I could recall was a little girl's heartbreak during a party hosted by her teenage brother and sister. After rereading the work, I realized that its significance for me came down to the story's title, which perfectly described my experience in the hospital.

*

For my school project on surrealism, I spent hours in the Donnell Library, known for its extensive art archives, pouring over books. Directly across the street was MoMA, where I could view some of the best examples firsthand or just wander the museum galleries and make my own discoveries.

Unfortunately, that wasn't the case for Giorgio de Chirico's painting, *Mystery and Melancholy of a Street*, held in a private collection. Like *Two Children Are Threatened by a Nightingale*, the work seized me and wouldn't let go even though I encountered it only in two dimensions, reproduced and bound into a book of art plates.

Eerie. Haunting. Desolate. Enigmatic. Unsettling. Again, there is a child, a girl rolling a hoop, her wind-blown hair and raised back leg indicating that she's in motion. But is she real? Was she ever real? She's been painted as a shadow of a girl, and she is moving in bright light down an empty street, maybe toward the source of that light. Up ahead looms the shadow of an oversized adult, who is probably not human but a statue.

Whenever I gaze on this painting, I feel in my heart and on my bones the heavy menace of its scene. To the girl's right is a circus box car, the rear door open to a dark, impenetrable interior. To her left are the repeating arches of a white colonnade, each entranceway filled with more shadow and unknown threats.

At the time MoMA exhibited this and 19 other de Chirico paintings in 1955, the exhibition director, James Thrall Soby, wrote:

> ". . . the figure of the girl is an unforgettable invention . . . One has the impression that even if she reaches the light, she is doomed, for she is herself a shadow, perhaps retracing the steps which led to her dissolution, her image invested with the horror of ghostly re-enactment. No other painting by de Chirico more piercingly conveys the sense of omen . . ."

*

When my playmates flung their dolls—uncombed or bald, filthy, one-shoed, sometimes naked—I felt myself shrink back. I wasn't happy about my reaction and took pains to hide it so that I wouldn't be seen as an outsider. My well-groomed dolls had too much self-possession and dignity to be neglected and tossed about and had given me the gift of their benign, predictable presence. Eventually they made room for a menagerie of stuffed animals—I remember a cat, dog, rabbit, tiger, lion, alligator and teddy bear, all safely residing in the Noah's Arc of my bed.

*

I hoped the nurse wouldn't notice me, occasionally peeking over the edge of the sheet. I hoped I didn't exist for her. If she knew I knew, would she give *me* the needle, too? "O.K.!" the boy had wailed back after her threat, "BUT PLEASE PICK IT UP!" Before long his pleas stopped and I heard only soft whimpers. Then—silence. Because of his exhaustion and defeat? Or at that moment, was the child hugging his bear? Was there mercy?

THE CLOAK ROOM

The very sound of it was foreign to our ears. Who wore cloaks? Vampires. Stealthy spies with hidden daggers. And men in top hats who appeared in movies and old-fashioned story books. Certainly no one we knew as first-graders at St. Joan of Arc—except, perhaps, for the nuns whose sleeveless black capes swirled in their hurried winter walks through the schoolyard to the convent. But their habits covered every inch of skin up to their necks; even their brows were partially obscured by fabric stiff as cardboard and white as their bony hands—the only other flesh exposed. On second thought, we couldn't really say we "knew" the nuns when their very bodies were concealed and their lives outside the classroom a mystery.

The cloak room, although part of our daily lives, held its own mystery. A narrow, dimly lit passage at the back of the classroom with a door on each end for entering and exiting, it was a kind of way station, a place to unbundle, to shed the layers in which our mothers swaddled us. Every morning Sister summoned us to the closet—first the boys, one row at a time, and then the girls, for no mingling of the sexes was allowed in that tight space. Above our teacher's desk, high on the wall, Christ hung, his feet and hands nailed to the cross. In this setting, our teacher's commands carried an authority that no one thought to question.

Once called, we would hastily remove the quilted leggings, cable-knit sweaters and scarves that covered our maroon uniforms and for the boys, their navy pants and white oxford shirts. In stormy weather, after taking off our boots, we'd sometimes feel tiny nail heads in the floorboards pricking our heels while we breathed the scent of dampness and old wood.

Our bulky outerwear exhaled winter as if alive, still animated by the recent presence of our young bodies, struggling to stay on the long rows of hooks, taking up more room than we did and sometimes falling to the floor in heaps. Even as a five-year-old, I'd hurry to restore order, coaxing my clothing back into position as if bidding farewell to the self I'd inhabited at home, the carapace I'd shed for the school day ahead. The maroon jumper and white nylon blouse with its prim collar were now revealed. That clothing lay close to my flesh but never in comfort. I think of my uniform now as an imposed disguise that cloaked whoever I was becoming. Then I stepped outside wearing the regulation brown lace-up oxfords that I despised and took my place at my alphabetically assigned desk, my hands tightly clasped and poised at its edge as we'd all been instructed to do on our first day.

I'll never know why I stayed behind with another girl in the cloak room that morning. As we lingered, I discovered the unprecedented pleasure, then joy, of not being missed—hide-and-seek without the seeking. We must have told each other stories, played some quiet games. As the minutes accrued, we gradually realized our predicament. The longer we stayed, the more difficult it became to leave—fear had invaded, turning our haven into a holding pen. I pictured the spectacle of our emerging while a lesson was underway, imagined our shocked classmates, the thunder-crack of the yardstick we had dutifully avoided. And with time came the dawning recognition of my infraction—or was it sin? My uncharacteristic spontaneity had made me a miscreant, a word I didn't yet know but felt instinctively.

The heavy coats of our 48 classmates brushed our faces, keeping us company in an intimate way that we hadn't ever experienced, a congregation of children surrounding us, dismissing our guilt. But our classmates were not with us—they were out there, beyond our sight as we were beyond theirs. We could hear only the sound of our teacher's heavy tread up and down the rows and feel our own quickened breath. No longer sprawled at play on the floor, we now stood side by side, our bodies tense. The next day, as Sister handed out test results, my co-criminal and I exchanged furtive glances, both shamed and relieved that we had missed a surprise quiz.

How we managed to slip back into our places without detection I don't recall. What I do recall is how frightening it was to be forgotten, how illicit that felt. And how thrilling: two "good" girls who could disappear.

UNDER THE RIVER AND INTO THE WOODS

My tiny fingers could not release the metal lock. I reached up on tip-toes, trying again and again, but the lock didn't budge, and I knew in my three-year-old pounding heart that, once more, I was trapped in the bathroom. Once more, my wish for privacy had eclipsed my fear of being alone in the small, white-tiled room.

Before long, I heard a commotion outside the door—a stranger's voice and my mother talking even faster and more emphatically than usual. Then the sound of banging moved to the hinges, growing louder, and within a few minutes, a New York City policeman loomed over me, a towering vision of navy blue and flashing metal badge. The last time I'd become a prisoner of my own making, my affable Uncle Charlie had been drafted to take down the door. But this was completely different. The surprise appearance of this authoritative stranger was enough to strike terror in me and put an end, once and for all, to my childhood lock-ins.

But that experience sowed the seeds for a lifelong tug of war. On the one hand, I had a persistent fear of being trapped in small spaces and suffocating (a fear exacerbated by childhood asthma). On the other hand, I descended daily into the subway, that infamous, no-escape "hole in the ground," with fearless New Yorker pride. In fact, negotiating tunnel passageways to transfer lines and riding deep under the East River have become second nature.

And there was also the conflict between my appreciation for nature, including the forest, and the anxiety I battled as soon as my feet left pavement. I couldn't help feeling that I'd inevitably become lost, and the woods would begin to close in.

As it happens, my life was threatened in both places, subway and forest. But to both I return.

When an un-air-conditioned train during a summer heatwave suddenly stalled inside an airless tunnel, all power to the motor, fan and lights cut off, bodies packed together, I verged on panic. Passing minutes felt like hours as we waited for some explanation over the intercom that never came. The stifling air seemed to press the ceiling down.

My face must have betrayed my stricken state because just as I was about to lose consciousness, a man rose and gestured towards his seat. The stars before my eyes faded when I bent my head very low between my knees. Observing myself across the distance of time, I see a kind of medieval supplicant bowing deep into the blackness. Eventually, power returned and the train groaned into motion.

This experience, frightening as it was, became just another personal subway tale. Although I felt very vulnerable at the time it was happening, I knew deep down that I would survive. But I had no such certainty on a ride years later as I sat in an almost-empty first car heading from Queens into Manhattan. In enclosed environments, I've learned to make myself small and self-contained as if to maximize what little space surrounds me. I've learned to immerse myself in the distraction of reading—and if the words are too disturbing, I stop reading lest my quickened breath consume more than my allotted share of oxygen.

That morning, I abandoned my book when several people suddenly rushed in from a car farther back, their faces white with panic. They were immediately followed by scores of other clearly terrified passengers escaping into the presumed protection of the motorman's car. "What's going on?" someone across the aisle asked. "There's a man back there with a gun!"—a sentence that stopped time in what until then had been the inexorable forward motion of my life.

I don't recall the faces, just the look of fear that pushed the fleeing men and women from the last car to the first—where they had to stop, having reached the beginning and maybe the end. Perhaps this was our Omega Train. We were in the long stretch of tunnel underneath the East River between the two boroughs, a five-minute ride. It felt like five hours though I'm certain the motorman powered the train to the maximum speed allowed, his hand never releasing its pressure on the blasting horn.

During those moments of horror, I didn't think about the weight that rooted me, the river pressing the tunnel walls and below the tunnel, the earth with its gaping mouth. I didn't see my life flash before my eyes. What I saw and remember are the plastic turquoise seats—how hard, ugly and oddly bright they were, built for human cargo, and how they would outlast us all.

When we pulled into the first station in Manhattan, I was relieved to be alive. That subway platform, 73 feet below street level, felt as refreshing as a windswept prairie.

Although I've never shrugged away this brush with death, I've probably over-compensated with a kind of psychic swagger: "I'm a tough New Yorker, I ride through a tunnel below the river nearly every day without fear."

You might think that the great outdoors—beaches, meadows, and mountains—are environments where fear never, or rarely, enters the picture for me. And you would be right. But forests? Here is where it gets complicated. I'm drawn to their majestic, primordial beauty, and when I'm on a well-marked trail, I breathe freely, absorbing every rustle and flash of birdwing. But as The Brothers Grimm taught me, a wild wood is more threatening than any environment imaginable—a primitive place set apart from civilization where strange and perhaps evil things can happen. Even on a sunny day, there is darkness and that existential "no exit" feeling for me. Strange as it may sound, a thin line of bright orange Cheez Doodles on a subway floor once reminded me of the breadcrumbs that Hansel and Gretel left in the forest to mark their way back. So in my mind, subway and forest have much in common, but the greater danger lies in the forest.

Against my better judgment, I once agreed to try camping out with my husband and some cousins. We were on a friend's land in Vermont over Columbus weekend, a time of year when the temperature drops well below freezing at night. That meant sleepless hours that I spent shivering from the cold, howls of animals on the prowl, and cracking twigs right outside our tent.

The next day, exhausted but unwilling to stay behind alone, I joined my companions on a nature walk.

Most of the trees were stripped bare. Dull mahogany-hued leaves clung to a few like tattered rags. And the birch trees that covered the mountainside appeared from the distance like bones picked clean.

The first few hours were pleasant enough. Once we decided to return, though, the mood grew somber as we found ourselves tramping in circles. There were no landmarks to guide us, and the more we tried to use reason to find the right direction back, the more every bush and rock and tree looked the same. After several hours, we had gone nowhere and we knew it. The wind had picked up and I wished I'd worn an extra sweater under my jacket.

Being lost in deep woods is like being trapped in a cell that even the jailers have forgotten. Every tree began to remind me of locked bathroom doors, looming and impenetrable. Rays of sun seemed to struggle through the treetops high above. I thought of prisoners facing the agony of a window so distant that no view out was possible and only filtered gray light penetrated.

The afternoon began to wane. Around us the colors changed, but not just because of the fading light. They appeared otherworldly and surreal, like the turquoise seats on that first subway car. It was a startling transformation that turned our innocent walk into a primeval leap into something unspeakable—perhaps our own impending deaths from exposure, hunger or thirst.

Eventually we stumbled our way out. Never before has the sight of blacktop awakened such a feeling of joy. After following the road for about a half hour, a farmer passing by in his truck stopped to give us a lift back. We had wandered miles from our starting point.

Despite these experiences, I don't consider myself claustrophobic under everyday conditions, just in extreme circumstances like the ones I just described. In fact, I can go for years without feeling my heart race and hands sweat with the fear of being trapped.

That's what occured during my first visit to Italy. I couldn't get over how well the dead and the living get along, citizens of the same city rubbing shoulders at every turn—the way the eyes of men framed in wall shrines would tenderly follow the widows who passed on their way home. And I couldn't get over the bathrooms, narrow as coffins, bathed in a kind of séance light. I feared the locks on those doors and stared as I might before abstract paintings, trying to figure out how the odd-looking pieces fit together to bring you in and then let you out.

But I might not get out until I'm found dead, I thought, trapped later in the cellar toilet of a café by the Bay of Naples, once more unable to budge the strange lock. It was a tourist trap of a place where old men shuffled about, selling roses, scratching out "Santa Lucia" on battered violins. A place where I expected to pay with lira, not sudden tears for the dead relatives I'd never met. Only a stranger, someone's grandmother calling to me what must have meant *Stay calm!* from the other side of that immoveable door could release me from my prison. I fell forward—the full, stiff weight of my body sprung into her warm, black haven.

SEARCHING FOR GEORGE, DAN AND FERGUS

George is in China now, buried there. Or maybe not. Maybe he was cremated, his ashes flung into Beijing smog—I'll never know. But one thing is certain: this son of New England is not in America. Alice, the woman who married him in his eighties as he began his decline, severed contact the frigid day that she had him carried onto a jet for the long journey back to her native land. "The acupuncturists' needles are longer in China," she offered as her only explanation for the move, in what would be our final conversation. Within a few weeks, on January 15, 2010, George was dead—88 years to the day after his birth.

His relatives erected a memorial headstone in their family plot in Northeast Harbor, Maine, on Mount Desert Island. I've read that it's a small cemetery in a forest near the harbor. Nothing lies below that slab but earth. I haven't been there, but I'm sure his name faces the sea.

*

George's ancestors were among the first Puritans to arrive on these shores. When I met him in his small apartment near Madison Avenue my first day on the job, I laughed to see an imposing black plaque on the wall above his bed. "Here lies George Peabody (1795-1869)" the archaic typeface declared—a replica, I soon learned, of the gravestone of his relative buried in Salem, Massachusetts. The cemetery borders his birthplace, the former town of Danvers; its citizens had renamed part of the town Peabody in his honor years before his death.

From the George Peabody I'd come to know, I learned that his ancestor was born into very modest circumstances but made a fortune, founding a bank for international monetary exchange that was the precursor of J.P. Morgan. "He gave all of his money away—more than eight million—and built housing for the poor in London," he said. I listened intently, and it would not be an exaggeration to say that I was awe-struck as the story unfolded. "When he died, he was so beloved that Queen Victoria sent his remains to America on one of her ships—after he had been interred for a month at Westminster Abbey. The body was handed over to Admiral Farragut in Maine, and a second funeral was held."

His tone was nonchalant, but it seemed that George felt it was important to let me, a stranger, know about his family history. I was 23, raised in the city's "outer borough" of Queens, and still unemployed two years after my college graduation just as the city was going bankrupt. This man was like no one I had ever met. For the next several years, until I found a full-time job, I worked a few days a week as George's administrative assistant, typing his PhD-thesis-in-progress on power in organizations and his correspondence with friends, business associates and colleagues worldwide. I answered the phone in the rare moments he stepped away and brewed the tea we sipped, working on opposite sides of his big, cluttered desk.

A gulf could have stretched between us—this hearty, sandy-haired man of 52 born two years before my father, an ordained Episcopal priest who had been director of leadership training for the church, who had traveled to ghettos across America with community organizer Saul Alinsky, author of *Rules for Radicals*, to learn what he could. This handsome, worldly man with a trans-Atlantic accent like Cary Grant's whom I'd mistaken for British when we first spoke on the phone (my first exposure to Boston Brahmin inflections). This man who visited my husband, Bill, and me in our newlyweds' ground-floor, alley-facing Bronx apartment and sat with us on the shag rug in his jeans and blazer, drinking three-dollar-a-bottle Spanish wine. This man of impossibly distinguished lineage who once posed in front of a park's long list of visitor restrictions, smiling for our camera while he "flipped the bird." He asked for a print of the snapshot, and I almost expected it to appear in his bathroom, next to the framed *New Yorker* cartoon of a dowager complaining to her husband, "Now that they've cracked the genetic code, I expect *everyone* will want to be a Peabody!"

*

My brother Bob spent endless hours researching our family roots using the Ellis Island website, but could find no record of anyone preceding our maternal and paternal grandparents. All were born in the neglected Mezzogiorno and, in the early years of the 20th century, joined millions of other southern Italians fleeing to America.

My paternal grandfather Salvatore Rotondi arrived here as a married 28-year-old, but died of pneumonia less than two decades later when my father Dalio ("Dan") was an infant. My grandmother Assunta, also from the Benevento province near Naples, attempted to manage their Bronx lumber and coal business by herself during the Depression, while caring for her daughter and six sons. Before too long, cancer took her life. My father, the youngest child, was sent upstate to Sparkill, to be raised at the St. Agnes Home and School run by Dominican nuns.

Despite the losses and deprivations of his childhood, my father embodied optimism and good cheer. At five feet eight inches, he wasn't a tall man, but he had the posture and bearing of someone raised by ego-bolstering parents who assured their child, "You can accomplish anything!" The reality was that no one had taken a personal interest in my father's future. None of his older brothers or sister earned a college degree—which he ultimately managed to achieve, becoming a teacher of industrial arts, English to the foreign-born at night, and, in his fifties, a special education teacher in Harlem.

I like to picture him in one of his favorite places, trolling a beach, eyes focused downward, stopping to lift up stones and shells for closer scrutiny. "*Wunderbar!*" he often enthused, a German word he picked up somewhere. When his bulging canvas bag began to overflow, he smiled over his treasure, to be used for one of his arts and crafts projects.

I also link George with the sea. I picture him in a loose navy-blue sweater on the sailboat he owned with one of his three brothers, explaining to me and Bill, the wobbly novices, about wind currents and nautical maps, the sun glinting off his tortoise shell glasses. This was a new role for me to absorb—George as confident, relaxed captain and commander. That one-time experience of sailing the Connecticut coast, sleeping onboard was, to me, as exotic and linked to social class as the images stamped in my mind of immigrants bedded down on city fire escapes in summer. My maternal grandparents, who headed to Carmine Street in Little Italy after their processing at Ellis Island, might have been among them.

*

My father lay in the hospital bed, consumed by the pneumonia that would finally release him from Alzheimer's disease, 12 years after his initial diagnosis at age 70. By the end, his eyes still held a flicker of recognition for my mother who visited every afternoon, staying into the evening, constantly monitoring his every need. But I don't think he knew who I was—his eyes, once so lively, were a void. And with this knowledge, I fell into my own void: the girl who reminded everyone of her father.

I had to climb out, make my own mental home movies: dad not even attempting to modulate his jubilation when he won a game of Scrabble. Dad talking to everyone, including the Jehovah's Witnesses who would ring our doorbell, invariably just as we were all about to leave together—he couldn't resist a spirited theological discussion. Dad unafraid to pursue a conversation into a debate over current events or a heated defense of exploited workers or blacks in America. Dad and my mother getting into a long argument about the "rightness" of marrying someone who wasn't of your race. The impassioned tone shocked my 11-year-old self because the subject was purely hypothetical for both.

*

When I flew for the day to Washington, D.C., where George had moved decades earlier, I knew it would be the last time I'd see him. Our friendship had been nurtured over the years through steady phone calls, his annual Thanksgiving visits to family in New York, and get-togethers when I occasionally traveled to D.C. for work.

Like my other close friends, George had a lively sense of humor that kept us connected. I've since learned that he was a descendant of John Endicott, the first governor of the Massachusetts Bay Colony and, according to historians, a "zealous Puritan." Endicott disapproved of "immodest dress in women" and long hair for men and banished those with unorthodox religious views. He also managed to have a few Quakers hanged. I wonder what he would have thought of George, a minister with not exactly an irreverent streak, but a quick laugh when it came to religion-as-synonymous-with-stuffiness. With 16 years of Roman Catholic education under my belt, I could always prompt a reaction by reciting the Baltimore Catechism like a speeded-up automaton or recalling Johnathan Edwards' sermon, "Sinners in the Hands of an Angry God," required reading at The Mary Louis Academy.

Alice, who had put an end to George's lifelong bachelorhood, answered the door at their apartment in the Watergate complex. After passing through the spacious lobby with its glittering chandelier, I felt I'd stumbled into the wrong place. The clean, orderly home I remembered had been obliterated; magazines, newspapers, framed art and documents and papers of all kinds covered the surface of every chair, table, desk, even the floor. The counter of the gloomy galley kitchen—some lightbulbs must have burned out—was littered with rotting apple cores.

In the twilight of his bedroom, the nightstand cluttered with pill bottles and sick room paraphernalia, George was being fed by an aide. He couldn't speak, but his still-bright blue eyes followed me as I crossed the threshold and approached his bed. I was certain that he knew me, that behind those eyes was not just awareness but intelligence. I found myself adopting the chatty cheerfulness of the broken-hearted. When I reminisced about a poetry reading of mine that he had loyally attended despite the stormy weather years earlier, quoting an amusing comment he'd made, George chortled, though weakly, at just the right moment. I felt encouraged until I wondered if his mental awareness made his physical breakdown that much more terrible to bear.

*

When my father saw children beyond the window of the nursing home that last year, his eyes would fill with tears. There was no way to understand why. Was he moved by the recognition of their innocence? Was he returning to himself as a boy, hiking miles to the local public school in winter, wearing ill-fitting shoes? I could only guess. In the deckle-edged photos taken during his older brothers' and sister's occasional visits, he wears a newsboy's cap, tweedy pants that are too large for him, and a big grin.

*

Fergus Anckorn, born in England in 1919, was taken prisoner by the Japanese when he was 23, an enlistee in the 118th Field Regiment Royal Artillery. A talented magician, he seemed to be a man who had managed to conjure his own survival. Bill and I met Fergus on a two-hour train ride from Bath to London in 1995, the 50th anniversary of the dropping of the atom bomb on Hiroshima. He had spent three years in a Burmese camp during the war—the war my father fought as a corporal in the 16th Armored Division that rumbled through Eastern Europe, and the war that George battled as a Navy officer at Iwo Jima. Fergus was a slave laborer on the infamous "Death Railway" being built as a supply route between Burma and Thailand, a project made famous through *The Bridge On the River Kwai*. He survived artillery shelling, a massacre at the Alexandra British Military Hospital (he covered his head with his bloodied sheet and played dead), and then, time in the prison camp.

There Fergus endured near-starvation and beatings as he attempted, using his severely injured leg and right arm, to drag logs inch by inch through unrelenting jungle. Always, he said, he kept the image of his fiancée Lucille before him and used his magician's sleight-of-hand to keep the camp commandant entertained. Fergus's mother called him "Smiler," and it is probably his belief in the impossible that kept him going when so many of his mates died.

A very articulate survivor, Fergus had prepared well for the interview he'd given to a TV reporter just hours before boarding the train. From his valise, he showed us war-time letters, photos and a postcard for his mother with a message hidden in shorthand that she decoded—he later became a teacher of shorthand and other business subjects.

"Keep smiling," Fergus said, as he stepped off the train at Paddington Station. Bill and I were shaken. After a few years had passed and I couldn't forget him, I wondered how we could have let Fergus vanish from our lives. The two hours spent in the company of this extraordinary man had upended my assumptions about human nature. I kept hearing his words, "But I hate no one. It was just the war." Although I didn't have an address for Fergus, I decided I had to track him down.

And then, I got very lucky: Hunter College, my employer, hosted a conference for international humanitarian workers being addressed by Great Britain's Lord Owen. Through a co-worker involved with the conference, I wrote to Lord Owen, describing our encounter with Fergus years earlier. In the envelope, I enclosed a letter to him in care of the Magic Circle of Magicians, remembering that Fergus was a proud member. Lord Owen informed me that he was forwarding the letter to the "Centre for the Magic Art" at its London headquarters. "I have been assured that this will reach Mr. Anckorn; my office having spoken to someone who was due to meet him that very evening," he wrote to my astonishment and gratitude.

Fergus replied within days, and we have stayed in touch since, at first through air-mailed letters and later via email. A few years ago I connected with his daughter, Deborah Cortey. "Here's her email address," he wrote. "Just curious why you want it." I don't recall how I danced my way out of that. I knew I couldn't say, "I need to know if anything has happened when your replies stop"—as they did for a long period just when my father's Alzheimer's disease was worsening and I feared the worst for Fergus, too.

*

Psychologists call it "anticipatory grief," this mourning before a loved one has died. My grief began the day of dad's diagnosis. Because he wasn't raised in a family but an institution, there were few stories of his childhood. I had only the man I knew who was slipping away from me, grasping for words that, more and more, eluded him.

*

George took pleasure regaling us with family stories. "My mother was given a Degas for a wedding present but too much bosom showed, in her opinion, so she gave the painting to the rummage sale of her favorite charity," he once told me, enjoying my shock. The one time we visited him at the Peabody summer retreat in Northeast Harbor, I was struck by the scene when we arrived: George sitting at an oversized desk, engrossed in his writing, while directly behind him, sailboats race on a cove's sparkling waters. The sprawling white clapboard home had been built in 1924 by his father, the Reverend Malcom Endicott Peabody, and remained as it was then, with original plumbing and claw-foot bathtubs. Window curtains that had been hung 50 years earlier were still "perfectly good," he said with a grin, quoting his mother. His Brooks Brothers shirt, as always, was faded and its cuffs frayed. To the Peabodys, extravagance was not a virtue.

*

My father found discards and made art from what others would call junk, using only his imagination, never a pattern or guide. A printing company's used plates sparked his Metal Period—all kinds of animal and human figures such as dueling knights suddenly began to populate our tables, the dining room sideboard and a desk top. It never bothered him, or me, that typeface and photos appeared on the reverse side of these creations, a seeming flaw that we felt actually added to their character. I never knew where he found the hollow metal tubes that he used to construct a slew of xylophones, which he taught himself to play in a rudimentary way. When a local paint store went out of business, its wallpaper sample books that he found piled up on the sidewalk became a mother lode of inspiration for collage. A lumberyard's cast-off scraps of circles, rectangles and irregular shapes led to his mature Wood Period, which produced an abstract, life-sized sculpture that I called "The Three Musicians." It was strongly reminiscent of Picasso's painting of that title, but his modesty didn't allow him to accept the comparison.

*

The war with Japan was over, but the prisoners didn't know that and were forced to stand 20 minutes before a firing squad. After suffering this final act of cruelty, they were released. Fergus weighed 74 pounds. "My stomach shrunk permanently," he told us. "I can't handle eating a big meal."

*

My father always ate with gusto, relishing every bite and often exclaiming his appreciation. I imagine that some people who grew up in an orphanage during the Depression might develop a taste for the finest food later in life if they have the means. But my dad's tastes remained simple and he satisfied easily, accepting my mother's burned steaks and soggy canned vegetables without complaint, even with good humor. As Alzheimer's began to stake a greater claim on him, I noticed that he ate quickly without pause or looking up, as if each meal would be his last. It seemed he was paying homage to hunger, head bowed almost to his plate, not raising his eyes until hunger left him. Then he would look up and smile, a small boy relieved.

*

When George found a lobster in a trap that he hadn't set himself, he took it, replacing the Crustacean in the wire cage with a bottle of good Scotch. "That's the time-honored tradition here," he said. Although I couldn't offer lobster, there is nothing I relished more than cooking a multi-course feast for George, who considered my ethnic fare a luxury, one he was happy to accept. I felt proud that any Puritan leanings he had toward frugal meals didn't stand a chance against my invitations, and I took great satisfaction in that. Invariably, I'd invite as many friends as my table could accommodate because I wanted them to experience him, to know for themselves the depth and originality of his thinking and to show him off a bit. George was as engaging as any guest of Anderson Cooper discussing politics, history and current events, but he never took center stage. Instead, he had the ability to draw people out and listened closely—a skill he may have developed as a priest, although in all the years of our friendship, I never saw him wear a collar.

*

To cook for my father from scratch was my gift to help erase his past deprivations. I planned elaborate menus: wild mushroom soup, chicken Marsala, pasta with fresh basil and tomatoes, baked asparagus Parmesan, fruit pies whose dough I rolled out, cut into strips and arranged in a lattice top, peach or blueberry bubbling through.

As a teenager battling my mother, who hated to cook, I bought my own knives and gadgets to prepare these meals. Strangely, the sturdy Army-issue fork from my father's mess kit remained throughout the years in a kitchen drawer with our everyday silverware but it was never used.

"Dad was in Europe during the Occupation," my brother told me when I phoned him to jar his memory, hoping to uncover missing parts of our father's past. "He said that the troops would eat outdoors, afterwards scraping the remains from their meals into a garbage can. The German civilians were starving, and dad told me he never forgot the sight of people fighting one another over the scraps."

*

George protested a proposal to build the World War II Memorial on the Washington, D.C. mall. I'm not sure why—he was fading then. I had begun to notice changes on those occasions when I was in Washington. A few times he became lost while driving, once heading in the wrong direction down a one-way street, and sometimes forgetting to make our dinner reservations. Then he had a bad fall, followed by surgery that his doctors declared a success but from which he never recovered completely. He grew more tentative on the phone, reaching for words, his once-hearty voice eventually diminishing to a whisper. Alzheimer's was ruled out, but no diagnosis could explain his continuing decline. By then, Alice, a Watergate neighbor and friend, had given up her own co-op and moved into George's apartment. On my final visit, despite the mess, I noticed on the wall an award for his World

War II service that I'd never seen and a newspaper clipping about a recent ceremony honoring him.

*

Dad talked about the war only when Bob badgered him for information. The Army decided that he should be trained as a medic, and my father speculated, half-joking, that they must have known he could stitch—leather belts and handbags that he designed himself. Bob had a more plausible theory: "Dad had poor eyesight, a big liability for the infantry. But on the plus side, he had a year of college, which wasn't typical of draftees at the time." (We both knew that my father had received a scholarship to attend Fordham University. But working two jobs to pay for meals and rent at a rooming house—one job as night shift elevator operator—he would fall asleep in class. Ultimately, he couldn't maintain the B average required to keep the scholarship.) My father was sent to Denver to receive extra training at Fitzsimons Army Hospital, where wounded men returning from the front were treated. He'd usually mention a particular lesson when tending to my bloodied knee or other childhood wound, but never described what he saw in service.

*

Before the start of George's memorial at St. James Church in New York City three months after his death, one of his surviving brothers mock-scanned the pews for the widow we all knew was absent, saying, "Are you here, Alice?" In the Gothic Revival splendor of the 19th-century church, we prayed psalms and sang hymns. A young man and woman who had met George in his capacity as a management consultant talked about his influence on their lives. Nieces and nephews fondly remembered their uncle, and some people with famous-looking faces whom I couldn't quite place told witty stories about young George's lust for life. I heard about debutante parties on a friend's yacht and something about a red sports car.

"He had such a spirit of fun," someone said and, in the silence of my thoughts, I agreed, recalling one of his many tales. One day, out for a pleasure cruise with a group of friends following behind, he invented a meaningless but portentous-sounding phrase, "The tomatoes are ripe," and relayed it by radio to the other boat. To his delight, they interpreted the words as secret code for the launch of a spy mission.

Political intrigue swirled in his circle: George's former brother-in-law, Desmond FitzGerald, a deputy director of the CIA under President Kennedy, had headed a task force to overthrow Fidel Castro (during the war, he was a liaison to the Chinese 6th Army in its campaign to take Burma back from the Japanese, perhaps helping to free Fergus). At one time, George was in contact with people on Block Island who provided a top-secret safe house for Daniel Berrigan, the anti-war Catholic priest fleeing a three-year prison sentence for destroying draft files. Given that history, cloak-and-dagger jokes seemed to come naturally.

During the memorial, as others continued to reminisce, I recalled an escapade of George at 15. "I was traveling with my family in Scotland for the Highland games, feeling bored," he had told me. "So I hitchhiked to Southampton and hid on a ship bound for America, but then got cold feet when I realized it would be a very tough swim from the boat to shore." He hitchhiked back to Scotland, where he located his family at a stadium, watching that day's competition. "Oh, so you're back, George," his older sister said off-handedly as he slipped into the seats beside them. (Marietta would go on to represent the U.S. on the United Nations Commission on Human Rights.)

I tried to imagine a similar unannounced adolescent escape from my family (first scenario change: they never went anywhere) without my mother making panicked calls to the police, sleeping by the telephone, and simultaneously organizing her own search party. I didn't know if the chasm in behavior was due to George's culture, so different from my Italian American background, or whether it hinged on wealth and class. I'll leave that to the sociologists, but for me, the story highlighted the huge contrasts in our backgrounds. George felt like a peer and a friend, and our friendship was all the more unlikely because of our differences.

After the memorial service, I didn't stay for the reception, realizing how difficult it would be to explain who I was and why I was there. We had just come together "In Thanksgiving for the Life of George Lee Peabody," and though I felt some comfort knowing how much he was loved, I was still the outsider, adrift. As the church's heavy doors shut behind me and I emerged from the darkness, blazing afternoon light seemed to stab my heart as if it were loss itself. I was both dazed and bereft. This was the same sensation that I had in London the summer we met Fergus. Bill and I had spent two hours underground in the Imperial War Museum, immersed in the somber tension of World War II and then—the sudden, disorienting brightness of present-day life on a city sidewalk.

*

At dad's funeral Mass, my cousin Richard read my poem, "With These Words," about how my father won my mother's love by writing to her every day from the front as his convoy moved east across Europe. She had saved some of these letters, tying the brittle bundle with blue ribbon. When I decided to release the bow to read them for the first time, my heart pounded in trepidation. In recent years, his halting words had dwindled to silence.

*

Fergus stopped driving after his last accident—his car was totaled, but born to "cheat death," in his words, he was uninjured and the hospital released him after just a few hours of tests. But his vertigo and unsteady gait—effects of wartime injuries catching up with him—have increased. He's moved from his home in Kent to an apartment near his son Simon. But Fergus still makes his monthly trips to London by railroad and taxi to attend meetings of the Magic Circle. Once the youngest inductee at 18, he is now the oldest. "I use a motorized chair to get around," he told me. "I'm a menace."

*

Can I still learn more about my friend George through his famous ancestor? "When I could still drive to the Magic Circle meetings, I always passed the Peabody buildings," Fergus recently remarked when I mentioned the name. "Of course I know him! What a great man."

For Fergus, the individual known as "the father of modern philanthropy" is alive in the legacy he left for the working poor—blocks of apartments where they could escape the Dickensian slums. Londoners have that tangible reminder, as well as Peabody Square with its statue erected in George's honor. But for me, the connection was only that humorously positioned grave plaque that I remembered from the first day that George Lee Peabody came into my life. I needed to do some hunting.

*

The full title of an 1870 biography by Phebe Ann Hanaford gets to the heart of the matter: *The Life of George Peabody; Containing a record of those princely acts of benevolence which entitle him to the esteem and gratitude of friends of education and the destitute, both in America, the land of his birth, and in England, the place of his death."*

Having never married, the 19th-century George gave away his enormous fortune for the public good. In America, he established the Peabody Institute in Baltimore, an intellectual and arts center; the Peabody Academy of Sciences in Salem; a coeducational teacher-training school in Nashville; as well as public libraries, historical societies, and archaeological and zoological museums. Reading the effusive prose celebrating Peabody, who began his career as a grocer's apprentice, I'm struck by the eyewitness accounts of his modest bearing, "his manner, that claimed no special attention or favors," and his easygoing way of speaking with everyone he encountered. I immediately thought of George, who asked questions and listened intently, whether he was communicating with a sales assistant or one of my friends.

Helping others was part of the family heritage, maybe the American version of noblesse oblige. My friend George's closest relatives, like himself, had been Episcopal priests. His grandfather, the Reverend Endicott Peabody, had founded the church-affiliated Groton School, renowned for its discipline and cold showers. It produced such alumni as Theodore and Franklin Roosevelt, senators, congressmen, corporate titans, and George himself, who, he complained— clearly still aggrieved—had received extra-tough treatment from his headmaster-grandfather. But earlier, the same Reverend Peabody had made history as the first Episcopal priest to serve the people of Tombstone, Arizona, visiting people in their homes and building a sizeable congregation in that rough mining town. George's father, the Protestant Episcopal Bishop of Central New York, had been a missionary in the Philippines. But "duty" to those less fortunate went much deeper, I learned in my first days with George, when he dropped family stories before me like breadcrumbs.

He was especially proud of his mother, Mary Parkman Peabody. In 1964 at age 72, urged by the Rev. Dr. Martin Luther King's Southern Christian Leadership Conference, she attempted to be served with black and white friends at a racially segregated restaurant in St. Augustine, Florida, aware that they would be arrested and jailed. "'We need some old people in this thing,'" she declared as she was taken away. She was held for two days and gave interviews from her cell. George's brother Endicott, then the governor of Massachusetts, called a press conference to praise his mother's courageous stand. The event made national headlines, led to a book, *Four for Freedom*, and helped advance the civil rights cause in America.

*

When Bob was 11 and I was eight years old, we took our first-ever family vacation—an extended weekend trip to the nation's capital. My dad had become friends with a teacher at his school whose church group was chartering a bus to Washington. Would we like to join them? Yes, we would. It was only years later that Bob and I realized how extraordinary that weekend was, for we were the only white people on the bus and in the downtown hotel where we stayed in that still-segregated city.

*

Sometimes I wonder if a man's worth is too often measured by the volume of material on the Internet related to his life. I Google my father and find his date of birth and death, social security number, former address and bare-bones army induction facts. No articles, biographies, quotes, obituaries, memories are on record. And strangely, despite his famous name, I find nothing about my friend George except for obituary and memorial notices.

But Fergus has been "discovered" by the media and is the subject of scores of features online, as well as two biographies: *Surviving by Magic: The Remarkable Story of Fergus Anckorn, Magician and Survivor of the Thai-Burma Death Railway* by Monty Parkin (May 2009) and *Captivity, Slavery and Survival as a Far East POW* by Peter Fyans (2011). In 2015, he played a key role in the BBC documentary, *Britain's Greatest Generation*, and appears prominently in its companion book. Right now, Fergus says, he is one of only two men alive from his regiment.

*

Bob calls to tell me something else about dad that I hadn't known: "When moving through Germany in the last stages of the war, the retreating soldiers told civilians that the Americans coming in would be plundering, raping and killing. Dad said he came upon an elderly German couple who were terrified of this prospect and had tried to slit their own wrists. He stopped the blood and bandaged them."

*

From one of Fergus's earliest letters:

> "I was stopped in the street yesterday by four young Japanese exchange students from a local school who were conducting some sort of survey, asking such questions as 'Can you name two towns in Japan? Can you name any Japanese food? Have you ever been to Japan?'

> So when they asked how I knew so much about Japan, I said to them—in Japanese—'I was a POW of the Japanese during the war.' Their mouths dropped, and they kept saying, 'Sorry, sorry, sorry.'

> I said, 'No—it's a long time ago. You are my friends.' I went into a shop and they found me and offered more copious apologies. I told them they were not born until forty years after these events, and I shook their hands and told them I was pleased to speak with them."

In a 2002 letter to me, Fergus wrote: "When I was a p.o.w. I had four ambitions if I should survive. To learn Japanese, to see Japan, to use a compass properly for tracking through the jungle and to learn to fly." He has accomplished all these goals. Three years later, he emailed: "In June, I took my son to Singapore and Thailand . . . to all the spots where something happened to me. None of those places exist now! Chunkai camp was deep in the jungle then. Now shops, buses, taxis and tourists. I have not had one nightmare since the trip. Not bad after 63 years of them every night!"

Fergus was feted with other veterans at the Imperial War Museum in 2005, the 60th anniversary of VJ Day, the victory over Japan, "a big to-do," he recounted, attended by Prince Philip, Lady Mountbatten, Dame Vera Lynn. For several weeks, he gave non-stop interviews to TV stations and the press. "I have become quite famous," he said, and though I couldn't see his face, I knew he said it in his low-key way, a mixture of pride and slight embarrassment. On June 26, 2014, he was invited to Buckingham Palace for another reception honoring the few surviving Far East veterans.

He has visited schoolchildren in Japan, met his former guards at a ceremony there and given talks about his experiences all over England. Most recently he has become friends with Konishita, a former Japanese guard on the Burma railway. Fergus met him at a "celebration party of reconciliation" between Konishita and Fergus's friend, also a Far East prisoner of war. "Konishita didn't want to be conscripted as a soldier and hated it," Fergus wrote.

When so much has been taken from him, how can he be so forgiving, I ask myself.

*

Almost daily, I'm reminded of bombings, beheadings, torture, slaughter in mosques, slaughter in a Texas and South Carolina church—and see hatred as an eternal presence, sometimes explosive, sometimes coiled quietly in a corner. But I'm also thinking of kindness. And the deeply human yearning for peace. And how these three men lived their lives.

*

In 1869, George Peabody spoke in public for the last time at
the National Peace Jubilee in Boston, a five-day musical festival
celebrating the end of the Civil War. Later that year, he died in
England. After his remains had drawn thousands of mourners to
Westminster Abbey, they were moved to one of Queen Victoria's
stately warships, flag at half mast, for the voyage to America.
"Humanity will note . . . her unaccustomed mission of peace and
sad courtesy," wrote a *London Telegraph* reporter. From France,
Victor Hugo paid tribute in a letter published in the *London Times*:
"Yes, America has reason to be proud of this great citizen of the
world and great brother of all men,—George Peabody. Peabody
has been a happy man who would suffer in all sufferings, a rich
man who would feel the cold, hunger and thirst of the poor . . .
On this earth there are men of hate and men of love: Peabody
was one of the latter."

I think the philanthropic George would have looked kindly
on his namesake, who quietly worked for peace. Social inequities
disturbed my friend, and that included the seemingly intractable
"troubles" in Northern Ireland, which he spoke about frequently.
He had traveled there often as a non-government-affiliated but
well-connected peacemaker, meeting with both sides, hoping
to negotiate an acceptable plan. The many letters I typed to his
contacts in Ireland left me with the impression that he wouldn't
give up trying.

*

Once my father began an arts project, he worked obsessively,
producing many versions. And then he gave away all of his creations—loom-knitted holiday wreaths and ornaments, hammered
copper scenes of prancing deer, enamel pins and pendants, original
string art. During several summers, he taught crafts at a public day
camp located in the classrooms and sticky-tar rooftop of a nearby
public school. At the end of each day, there was usually a pile of
left-over American cheese and peanut butter sandwiches, which
my father brought home and tried to foist on our neighbors, to
my embarrassment and Bob's. "I just can't bear to see good food

thrown out," he explained. By summer's end, there were few takers. The birds ate well.

*

I see my father by the shore. And I see him astride his omnipresent "stitching horse," an essential component of his leatherworking. The contraption stood several feet tall, had four wooden legs and a seat he would straddle for hours, sewing hides held by a clamp where a horse's bit would be. He sat there stitching my mother's stylish, extra-wide belts during their first years of marriage in an East Harlem apartment, and he sat there stitching the flower child purple suede vest and fringed shoulder bags that rarely left my body during my college years. He had built it himself as a young man—even the seat was thickly padded with genuine leather—and brought it along when moving into two other rental apartments and finally a house of my parents' own in Queens.

The stitching horse was an object of both fascination and joy for me as a child. Fascination, because even at a young age, I could lose myself watching my dad plunge the needle into the tiny holes he had pre-punched into the leather, observing his concentration as he manipulated the skin and the outlines of the finished belt or bag began to emerge, all the while patiently answering my questions. And joy because, when my dad had completed his work, I had free reign to mount it and play cowgirl just as other, less-fortunate children, might ride on a much smaller, store-bought hobbyhorse. Many years later, when my father must have sensed he would no longer be doing leatherwork, he gave away his stitching horse to a talented young man he'd met who couldn't afford the hundreds of dollars needed to buy a new one.

II. OBSESSIONS

MY BROTHER'S GUNS

My cousin's eyes are blazing as he turns to me and Bill. "Those two guys are going to kill us in our tents tonight," he says.

My first camping experience. We're in Vermont over a Columbus Day weekend on the land of our absent friend Vinny. I'm keeping my husband company as the camera on its tripod records the imperceptible nighttime movement of the stars. Peace. Love. Tranquility. Until the mood is shattered by Ron's passionate certainty that the two young strangers—unexpected intruders we'd encountered on this private land—are our murderers-in-waiting.

I picture a hunting knife slashing top to bottom through our canvas in a single, practiced motion, steel glinting like those stars, life's dazzle suddenly extinguished. No. Can't happen.

Discovering the men's presence soon after our arrival was a bad omen. Anticipating a family adventure—even an idyll—on our friend's 150 unspoiled acres, we were jolted by the incongruous blaring of acid rock. Leaving our clearing to investigate, we came upon the source: a tape deck blasting full volume from an open-doored, dented Chevy and two scruffy men in jeans unrolling their sleeping bags. Ron must have been more upset than he let on when their German Shepherd tried to attack his sweet-natured dog Jedgar. Canine violence was avoided just in time when the teeth-baring aggressor, sharply rebuked, backed off.

Still, hadn't we just shared our campfire for cooking when those guys entreated us after their fire died, leaving unbaked potatoes? At that moment, they seemed like next-door neighbors asking to borrow a cup of sugar. Hadn't we passed them plastic cups filled with our Burgundy and later, shared a joint and mellow conversation? It turned out that Mack and Chester were Vietnam vets, reputed friends of Vinny who, they said, had invited them to camp on his land any time. When they said goodnight and disappeared over a nearby hill, I felt only serenity and good will.

But Ron doesn't stop pacing back and forth before our dying fire, repeating his awful prediction, demanding that we wake up my brother Bob and his wife while he wakes up his family. "Let's pack up right now and drive home," he says. "You have to understand—our lives are at stake!"

I couldn't ignore those darting eyes, which projected a sense of doom and nervous energy that penetrated the core of his being. Bill tried reasoning. I couldn't absorb the words because at that point I was beginning to doubt my own rationality. Although a defender of logical approaches, I'd never dismissed the importance of hunches or intuition.

"O.K.," I hear Ron finally respond. "We won't wake them up. But that means I'll have to keep watch all night." And then I hear him say:

Let's get Bobby's guns.

My brother, blissfully asleep throughout this unfolding drama, had packed several rifles from his collection for target practice.

Now instead of envisioning our bloody massacre by knife, I envision Ron as some kind of Stone Age protector armed with a rifle instead of a rock by his side, quick to pull the trigger if one of those guys happened, in all innocence, to show his face.

Thankfully, the guns, which Bob had kept locked in his car, stayed out of reach. And so instead Ron fed the fire, a dedicated sentry for the next hour or so until he retreated to his tent without a word. I managed to survive—despite the sub-freezing temperature, animals howling, ominous sounds of crunching just outside our tent, a body wracked with cold and a mind vacillating between calmness and a single, terrifying thought: what if Ronnie is right?

The stars survived, too, a wispy trail of light that arced above us unseen until weeks later when they slowly appeared on paper in our closet-darkroom.

That experience is behind me. But decades later, the words "Let's get Bobby's guns" explode in my mind, releasing a toxic cloud of what could have happened that night.

*

My brother, then the owner of more than 100 guns and a few thousand rounds of ammunition, is a myopic CPA and professor of accounting and business now retired from a military college in Vermont. A Latin and classical Greek scholar with a Jesuit education and two graduate degrees, Bob shatters the stereotype of a good ole boy in love with his firearms. How many CPAs are equally at ease holding extra-fine-tipped pens and Smith & Wesson Magnum revolvers? And who can recite the latest tax codes and also identify the make and model of every gun he sees on TV westerns, mysteries and police series?

Born with the soul of General Patton, he was fascinated with guns and warfare even as a young child. One of my earliest memories is kneeling at the age of four beside my seven-year-old brother, praying that he'd find a tank under his bed the next morning. This was his most fervent wish—not just at Christmastime—and although every morning he remained tankless, we kept petitioning heaven, which makes me complicit in his earliest request for a potentially lethal instrument of warfare.

My lifelong love for my only sibling has always been mixed with a lifelong failure to understand his obsession. In the past decade, my unease has only grown. One in three Americans owns a gun, an armed citizenry unlike any in the world. In states like Arizona, anyone over the age of 18 can buy an assault rifle, which gun sellers instead call "military-style rifles," thinking that the change of language removes the stigma. As we know from recurring headlines, mass shootings with those rifles, whatever they are called, are tragically commonplace. In fact, according to the Centers for Disease Control (CDC), there is now one mass murder every day in the U.S.—not committed by foreign terrorists but Americans.

What is the source of this fascination that's never waned for my brother? I keep asking myself this question, knowing there's no logical explanation. We grew up in New York City in a state with some of the strictest gun restriction laws in the country. Our father, like most males of his generation, served in World War II but wouldn't reveal much about his experience in Europe despite Bob's questions. No one in our family hunted or owned firearms unless you count the BB guns that our cousins Ron and Richard shot in their backyard with Bob by their side. I used to joke that, like Bernard Marx in Aldous Huxley's *Brave New World*, Bob must have had "too much alcohol in his blood surrogate" during the embryo stage.

But society's influence can't be dismissed. Growing up in the post-war fifties, Bob read war-themed comic books like "G.I. Combat" and watched movies featuring John Wayne and most-decorated combat-soldier-turned-actor Audie Murphy. Those propaganda films glamorized the heroes of war and avoided real-life depictions of gushing blood and mangled limbs. He was also a loyal fan of all the 1950s westerns glorifying guns: *The Rifleman*, *Maverick*, *Gunsmoke*, *Tales of Wells Fargo*, *Have Gun, Will Travel*, *Wanted: Dead or Alive*, and on and on. In the sixties, one of his favorite TV shows was *Combat*, a more realistic portrayal of a World War II platoon in Europe. And yet, millions of male baby boomers watched the same movies and TV shows but left their gun fascination behind—so the power of pop culture can't be the only explanation.

By the time he was nine, Bob had discovered Kaufman's Army & Navy store near Times Square, a boy's paradise of army surplus. He began on a small scale by saving his allowance to buy military badges. When Bob's eighth grade graduation approached, Ron convinced my parents that Bob, an honors student bound for a Jesuit prep school, was mature enough to own a gun.

"Ron told me to close my eyes and when I opened them, I saw a J.C. Higgins bolt action one-shot rifle," my brother recalls. "It was one of the happiest days of my life." I'm certain he's not exaggerating.

What does a 13-year-old do with a rifle in New York City? He shoots. Inconceivable today is the fact that Bob and a friend from Maine, also 13, carried their rifles, in cases, onto the subway, heading for a shooting range in the basement of an industrial building in downtown Manhattan.

By the time he was 16, he had stockpiled inert hand grenades, mortar rounds, practice bombs, helmets, canteens, bayonets, dummy machine guns, bullets, and half a dozen rifles. Among them was an M-1 semi-automatic 8-shot that he bought for $80, having saved up from his $1.25-an-hour summer and weekend jobs.

When I reached that age, the counter-culture hippies were planting daisies in gun barrels, and my bedroom adjoining Bob's sleep-in arsenal was decorated with psychedelic posters. I didn't then and don't now understand Bob's obsession.

*

As a homeowner in Queens, Bob turned his finished basement into a hands-on Museum of Warfare. In one corner stood a 1907 World War I machine gun pointed towards the sofa and easy chair. In the back room, an inoperative washing machine became the target for shooting practice with an AR-15 rifle. To avoid nearby neighbors' detection and inevitable complaints, he covered up the blasts by simultaneously cranking up the booming finale of *Victory at Sea* on his stereo. Displayed on his basement walls were guns ranging from antique to modern. Deep-grained, ivory-embellished firearms handcrafted hundreds of years ago rested beside the ugly black plastic, purely functional weapons of modern warfare. Bob says that he enjoys knowing the historical aspects of older guns, but he clearly cherishes them all, reciting distinguishing characteristics and capability the way a father might boast about his child.

Soon he joined the Queens Pistoleers Club and then met the stringent requirements for a New York City pistol permit. Next came membership in the NYPD Auxiliary Police. After training, he accompanied cops on weekend, two-man foot patrols out of his local precinct.

*

In the late seventies, Bob was hired by Norwich University, the nation's oldest private military college. It had a tank or two on campus for Bob's pleasure—a better-late-than-never gift—and on the job, he wore a military uniform, had the rank of captain, and was saluted by cadets. Through Norwich, he went on occasional overnight "field training exercises" where he fired military weapons, flew in helicopters, and drove Humvees and even tanks, which I think of as a kind of Disneyland war simulation. In Vermont—a state where even Bernie Sanders defends gun possession—Bob acquired a Federal Firearms Dealer license. This allowed him to buy guns for himself at wholesale prices while selling to friends, neighbors, the military and police. At one point, he owned 175 modern firearms, including Glocks and fully automatic weapons, along with 10,000 rounds of ammunition. His gun collecting "hobby" had reached its apex.

At the age of 50, still a professor and CPA with tax clients, Bob decided he wanted to also work as a part-time police officer— not a volunteer or auxiliary but a real member of the force. I was aghast. My mother, not surprisingly, was apoplectic. "Why would he want to put himself in danger? What's wrong with him? What's the point?" Why, why, why? But Bob was determined. He attended the Vermont Police Academy—150 hours of courses and 100 hours of on-the-job supervision with a training officer of the Berlin, Vermont Police Department, all without pay. After serving for years as the official armorer of the Berlin force, he had finally joined their ranks. I'm glad I never saw Bob on duty, ready for action, carrying his .45-caliber Glock, pepper spray, baton, two sets of handcuffs and two-way radio. I'm not sure I'd have been more nervous if I'd seen him posed on a tank in army fatigues and a helmet.

For ten years, he kept this up. When he wasn't in the classroom lecturing on gross domestic product and risk and return, he was dealing with domestic violence calls, store break-ins, druggies and violent, raving drunks. Although he acquired the nickname of "Bob the Schmoozer" for his ability to find the right words to calm agitated people, he sometimes arrived on the scene with his gun drawn.

What was the return for him on so much risk? I don't understand.

*

THE SHOOT

Grackles swoop down, then spread
like a black cape around my brother's house.
My brother is kind to animals,
shoots at nothing but one man—
a perp line-drawn on paper, plucked
from his basement arsenal. I see that face
in fields of feverfew, pock-marked
by bullet holes.

When we meet, we never flout the rules,
avoid politics, the NRA, or why
a teacher would become a cop
in middle age. Instead, we hike his woods,
past ancient cars pushed down a ravine
by agents unknown. Their shapes shift
and sink, a growing mystery
in the forest bed. As we stroll the abandoned
road, I'll note its widening rift,
the new guns. *This one's a 22,*
my brother says and cocks his head,
making room for mine.
The scope snags a woodchuck
and bees that cling to raspberry fuzz.
One by one, the residents of his kingdom
pass through the crosshairs unharmed,
and yet I recoil when Bob takes aim.

He squeezes the trigger:
The cape explodes into shadow
that covers us both, then shreds to tatters
headed for my heart's chamber.

*

The National Rifle Association is renowned for its powerful lobbying against any regulations that would limit a person's ability to buy guns, whether it's a hunting rifle or an assault weapon. Parkland, Florida. Las Vegas. Pulse Orlando nightclub. Virginia Tech. Sandy Hook Elementary School. Columbine High School. San Bernardino. Fort Hood, Texas. No matter—the NRA ignores the horror of these slaughters and remains resolute in its mission to advocate for gun rights and against gun control.

The NRA's power over lawmakers is legendary. Although the organization was founded "to improve marksmanship and teach firearms competency and safety"—who can argue with that?—its intransigence toward any kind of gun ownership restrictions makes it Public Enemy No. 1 in my mind. I don't express my opinion to Bob, a longtime member of the NRA, which has certified him as a Pistol, Rifle, Shotgun and Home Safety Instructor. The shooting range that he set up on his land has been the site of NRA course instruction that he's given to Norwich's cadets and civilians.

"I became a hunting instructor so people would shoot safely," says Bob, who doesn't hunt but whose land is sometimes trespassed during hunting season. "And it's fun to target shoot. Anything can be a weapon. I resent that a gun is automatically called that."

And yet guns are the third leading cause of death among children according to the CDC. The majority of gun deaths in children were homicides—gun as weapon. Between 2007 and 2014, suicide by gun increased 60 percent—gun as weapon turned against the self.

Knowing that I'm writing about his gun fascination—a subject I've long avoided and am still loathe to probe deeply—Bob sends me emails filled with details, chronology and web links for more information. He is, after all, an accountant and teacher. A recent email begins, "I love this quote," and it's followed in 20-point, blue type: "'March 5, 1836: God Created Men and Sam Colt Made Them Equal!' (Old West Adage)."

He goes on to explain the appeal: When Condoleezza Rice, secretary of state under George W. Bush, lectured at Norwich University, she described the sense of safety that guns gave her and her parents—protection against hate groups like the KKK who might terrorize them in the Alabama backwoods where they lived. "The police, who were white and probably wouldn't care, were miles away and there were no telephones," said Bob. "She was firmly a Second Amendment supporter and was taught to safely handle guns at an early age."

Protecting oneself and one's family are the operative words for gun owners, who believe that if more people had firearms, society would be safer. It's rugged individualism writ large, easily fulfilled at the local Walmart, one of America's largest gun retailers.

*

PASTORALE

In the war game of chess,
kings and pawns know their place
on the board and space
themselves neatly apart. Mess

is not the military way
of course, which is why the field
around my brother's house, filled
with vintage army trucks, stayed

regimentally calm. Still,
there was something disquieting
to see all that armor fight
for attention, vying with frilly

ferns among the lilies, the kind
that bloom and die in a single
day. Visiting, I'd raise two fingers
in salute—half in jest to rile

Bob, but half in deference
to war's mysterious, lifelong grip
on him, a child conscript.

Our worried parents held conferences

on what might be the cause,
then gave up, bought him *Jane's*
Fighting Ships as a birthday gift. Insane—
a boy of eight who knew the force

of every Gatling gun and quoted
General Patton by heart. The radio van,
Vietnam jeep and cargo truck, crammed
once with men, have long been sold.

Only armored beetles live there
now. I imagine them in a march
to his shed where even parched,
dusty air can't dull the glare

of cherished brass: mortar shells
from our father's war lined
up by size in gleaming rows. Find
out the reason he clings to this. *Tell*

me why! Our voices rise, echo
present and past in this valley—
like ricochets that sully
the air, or words ending in blows.

                                        *

I'm in Vermont at Bob's place, peering through the crosshairs of a
Remington semi-automatic .22 rifle. In the meadow, an angry-look-
ing man dares me to shoot at his face, printed in black ink on
thin target practice paper that Bob stockpiles in his basement. I
squeeze the trigger, aiming. The blast echoes, filling the valley as
birds take flight.

    I'm struggling with a bad case of cognitive dissonance in firing
a gun. Holding it feels surreal. How could this object of such personal fear and loathing be in my hands? I feel the smooth wood,

peer awkwardly into the scope. In the spirit of sibling love after a long absence, I agree to give it a try. After my first miss, that face on the target seems to be sneering at me. I steady my arm against the deck railing, squint, and pull the trigger again, just as a vivid memory returns. I'm drawing a plastic gun from a holster slung around my red corduroy, white-fringed cowgirl skirt. Bob and I are playing shootout games in our parents' tiny apartment in Queens.

This time my bullet grazes the target near the man's temple. Better, but not good enough. I can feel tension rising in my chest, spreading down my arms and into my fingertips. The next time I shoot, I'm way off the mark. The shell falls to the ground, useless and spent, exactly as I'm beginning to feel.

But I'm feeling angry too, like a woman wronged by that leering SOB, like Thelma and Louise before they drove off the cliff, and I suddenly recall what it was like to ride the crowded subway as a young woman, pressed into, grinded against, too embarrassed to utter a word, every morning and after-work commute begun with trepidation, and I'm thinking *I will get him this time!*

I surprise myself by recognizing the heady power of holding that rifle in my hands, a feeling at that moment undiminished by any internal political monologues. I aim ever so carefully, stilling my emotions to a dead calm while knowing deep down that this is just a game.

My bullet rips through one eye. "You got him!" exclaims Bob, as if reading my mind. But now it looks as if the salacious creep is winking at me—like the drunk on the sidewalk who once grabbed my crotch, leaving me frozen on the spot, shaking with silent rage. I take up the rifle and carefully, methodically, fire.

A LESSON IN TIME

Against the wall, the moon face of a grandfather clock frowned. From that wall, the frown faced us. The clock was a staunch ally of my mother, perpetually anxious that she would be late, or that we (me, my dad, my brother) would arrive two minutes late to an appointment. The clock was her unlikely ally, tipping sideways slightly as if it had imbibed too much Colonial-era rum. And ironically, it kept terrible time. I'd try to read its face, but knew its face could not be trusted. I'd hear a faint ticking, but the sound was like a struggling heart in need of a pacemaker. Despite its infirmities, the clock, nearly seven feet tall, loomed over us, a bullying reminder of time's dominance.

Philosophers and rogue physicists continue to debate the very existence of time. What does "now" mean when it's become the past as soon as it hits consciousness? How can the present be measured if it is continually slipping into the future? And when we set our clocks ahead to Daylight Savings Time, what happens to that lost hour? You're in la-la land while time leaps ahead from 2 am to 3 am like a thief clutching his precious bounty who needs to disappear fast. Waking to a strangely dark morning, you ponder what cataclysm has befallen the world.

But such questions didn't come up at home because time wasn't a slippery abstraction but an omnipotent ruler over our lives. "When your time is up, it's up," Mother would say. Her obsession with time and her other obsession for objects from other eras came together in that clock, an imposing antique that, I'm sure she believed, lent a feeling of Old World solidity to our home. My mother's fixation on present-moment time and on anything "vintage" wasn't a contradiction. After all, antiques are survivors of time past, existing in the now, and their imperfections—a crack in a doll's porcelain face, the powdery leather cover of a gilt-edged book—stand out, asserting themselves and their ability to impede time.

And so our living room had that domineering clock and a clutter of uncomfortable Victorian chairs where none of us sat for more than five minutes. If you leaned back, your skull would encounter un-pillow-like carved wooden putti. They were fat cherubs with enlarged heads and hollow, demonic eyes who knew how to exert pressure in exactly the right spot, forever banishing any attempt to relax. After all, the word "slouch" is close to "sloth," and that deadly sin, lolling around all day in a soiled nightgown, never gave a thought to time. So sloth was banished from home. Bob and I were swift, we were alert—good soldiers who followed time's orders, communicated via the sergeant-at-arms, our mother.

Because of the unreliable grandfather clock, we turned to timekeepers we could depend on, our Timex wristwatches and the plastic clock radio on the kitchen shelf that Mother kept tuned daily to "The Make Believe Ballroom." The very name of that music program conjured up a fantasy life where time stood still as glamorous dancers swirled about in each other's arms. For hours the music played, counterpoint to my mother's floor scrubbing and furniture buffing and the unstoppable hands of that clock radio. During the day, time was always ahead of us, forcing a struggle to keep up.

Night was another story—isn't it always? The ticking on my bedside table often kept me awake, every audible second replaced by the next, the next, the next, each tick striking my ear drum like water drops against the forehead used to induce madness. Scientists claim that a life span is a billion heartbeats. Before long, the sounds entered me—no wonder the heart is called a "ticker." As seconds dragged into minutes, then hours, I felt the draining away of any sense of control over my life. I felt my life suspended. No, its slow unwinding in the dark, my allotted billion beats diminished. I felt the dark without and the dark within, the stifling, sealed chamber of insomnia.

As if through a keyhole, I'd watch myself float through the day just passed, but everyone I spoke with or encountered was like a ghost, and I was spectral, too, all of us characters from a place and time that may never have existed. At some point, I felt the ennui of watching myself as a stranger, and surrendered to sleep. That is, until the alarm sounded its warning: daylight has arrived. Do not be late.

Instead of time being on my side, it was on my back, a burden I've carried throughout my life. Two hours before a meeting, especially with a God-like authority figure such as a doctor, my mother would begin to harangue her "Hurry up's"—no grace period allowed.

As a child, the reprieve came on New Year's Eve. For once, bedtime was ignored so that my brother and I could watch the Times Square revelers on TV, all eyes on the blazing-bright clock tower. I didn't have the words then, but felt time's power over its subjects in the street, the millions of us watching clocks across America, the millions more counting the seconds worldwide. Time was in charge, invisible but relentless—no wonder my mother paid it homage.

"Five. Four. Three. Two. One!!" The frustration and occasional anger I felt having to kowtow to the dictator all year long gave way to the primal relief of pot-banging with metal spoons and the clanging of pot lids, a cacophonous percussion that was both an admission of time's supremacy and a joyful resistance: "Screw you, Time, and get lost!"

Maybe it was a kind of perverse resistance years later that lay behind my attraction to antique watches. I appreciated them as aesthetic objects, knowing they were practically useless but always hoping I'd find one that could literally be brought up to speed. I've lost track of how many dollars I've spent on a 1905 Rolex that didn't keep accurate time much more than six months after its repair, usually soon after the warranty had expired. By the end of the day, it would lose five minutes, then by the next week, six or seven —what I might not immediately notice, but what could get me in trouble if I didn't check the reliable watch I kept out of sight.

What do you expect from a woman who wears a blurry-faced man's watch more than a century old? Does the watch make the woman? Did mine say "Laggard. Nostalgia-lover. Luddite. Unfit for fast times?" Years later, I'd glance at my cell phone for the right time. If I'd been born in the fourteenth century, I'd probably have been the type to carry more than one hourglass in my basket, just in case.

In Gary Shteyngart's *New Yorker* piece, "Confessions of a Watch Geek," he introduced me to a world of Very Serious watch collectors. Members of the cult invest thousands of dollars on their status-name time pieces—both vintage and new models designed by Bauhaus-influenced artists. They spend hours on watch connoisseur websites, proudly post watch selfies on their forums, and meet in the back rooms of secret, no-address bars to discuss their latest acquisitions, which are passed around and examined to much admiration and envy. Reading this, I realized that the world of Shteyngart's "watch idiot savants" (his words) was not my world. Some of my watches were Timex and Bulovas, never the type to claim status or compete with chronometers for fractional-second accuracy like the ten-thousand-dollar models.

Shteyngart's essay on the watch as sexy status symbol reminded me of when models showed up in several fashion magazines the same month wearing two watches on one arm. I couldn't help being reminded of clocks set to the time of the world's capitals that you might see in an international bank. Did the double-watch say "I'm in New York but my second watch is set to French time, where my boyfriend is inspecting his Pinot Noir vineyards? Or I need to know London time so that I can instantly relay my buy/ sell orders to my broker in the City"?

Meanwhile, my mother, a dedicated flea-market enthusiast and collector, continued to bring home watch after watch, from sleek Art Deco to square-faced men's models to delicate evening watches encrusted with diamonds. What was the fascination? Did the time pieces signal a person with responsibilities, plans, important appointments? I suspect that I may be reading too deeply into this, and the appeal for my mother was probably purely aesthetic—my inherited downfall.

Mother generously let me choose the watches that caught my eye. In my freshman year of college, I sported a pink-strapped Disney watch, thinking it would hint at the hidden, playful side of a personality easily misjudged as "very serious." Minnie Mouse kept perfect time, and I was never late for class. In my early adolescence, knowing I'd major in English, I'd scribble poems with portentous lines like "I see time's shadow fall on all of us," as if we were walking sun dials. Then when I actually became an English major, my favorite poem was "The Love Song of J. Alfred Prufrock," partly because Eliot, unlike Mother, asserted, "There will be time . . . there will be time." The irony he intended by these words didn't dilute my pleasure.

THE SPANISH SHAWL

Magic the shawl that kept caressing and slipping sensuously down my bare, 20-year-old shoulders—a garment possessed but impossible to hold.

I haven't looked at it for many years, but I see it clearly in my mind's eye: gold silk, deeply fringed, and embroidered with multicolored flowers, bought in Granada on my honeymoon. In Europe for the first time, living on $20 a day, we were on a month-long journey across Iberia. I knew I wanted something transcendent that, in the future, would transport me to that time.

The new Spanish shawls displayed on racks in the town square were too expensive. But others were arrayed on white cloths over the ground like the sumptuous bounty brought home by an explorer from long, exotic travels. Silk can't have a patina, but it seemed to me that the shawl I chose had a depth and richness the new ones lacked. And it was priced lower because it had been "pre-owned." By how many generations? For how long? The questions drew me to it all the more. I imagined the shawl that was now mine once worn by a beautiful flamenco dancer, perhaps pulled tight against the sirocco years earlier by her equally ravishing mother. Its mysterious provenance shimmered.

The Spanish shawl has accrued the power of a talisman to me. It is the youth and passion of a very young couple beginning life together, as well as the fierce and sometimes dark beauty of Andalusia. It embodies the sum of new experiences: dipping fingers into the bubbling waters of a carved Alhambra fountain. Eyes sweeping across acres of giant, nodding sunflowers. Stalling, and then breaking down, in the Sierra Nevada mountains. Sitting inside a café in a border town at dusk, dogs wandering in like bachelors sniffing the air for action.

For many years, I wore the shawl only to weddings, a good-luck charm whose aura might touch the newlyweds. Eventually, I placed it at the bottom of a bureau drawer, where my buried treasure has remained undisturbed. I don't know if the fabric is growing fragile, once-bright threads rotting like Ms. Havisham's wedding dress, a disturbing metaphor, I admit. I can't help thinking that if I were to expose it to the air and light of the twenty-first century, it would crumble before my eyes like ancient Roman frescoes discovered during digs.

And so my Spanish shawl stays out of sight. I wear it in my imagination, walking medieval streets in relentless summer sun with my husband. A man sweeps the cobblestones with a bramble broom, two children leaping by his side. Down another narrow street, an old woman sewing in the shadowed doorway of her home looks up the instant we snap her photo. That night, as dancers swirl their skirts and stamp their feet on a tiny stage, we'll clink goblets of Rioja, and the wine will feel like a life-giving elixir.

BEAUTY, TRUTH AND GLOVES

The lights have dimmed, strings and horns swell ominously, and a gloved hand looms: murder is in the air. And because of those gloves, the hapless forensic scientists will come up empty after dusting for fingerprints at the crime scene. Between all the murder mysteries I've been watching lately, supplemented by scores of noir film classics starring vamps in black satin, elbow-length gloves, I've been under a spell.

Gloves=Death? Why not? Just ask dueling victims Alexander Hamilton. Or Elizabethan actor Gabriel Spence, done in by none other than playwright Ben Jonson (serious artistic differences?). Or Alexander Pushkin. Or so many others. The beginning of the end for them was a glove flung to the ground. Before they knew it, they were counting off paces and aiming their pistols—but not accurately or fast enough to avoid becoming history's ultimate losers.

My interest in gloves, approaching obsession when it comes to my own collection, is nearly lifelong. On the surface, they would seem to be a superficial object of attraction. Would a psychologist say that I'm avoiding skin-to-skin contact by the wearing of a second epidermis? Hardly. So, what else would account for my fascination? I haven't found the answer, but I was glad to learn recently that I'm not alone.

What a relief to discover like-minded souls in the Worshipful Company of Glovers of London, which traces its origins to a medieval trade guild. In 2013-14, celebrating the 375th anniversary of its Royal Charter from King Charles I to promote "the wearing of gloves and the business and training connected with glove making," the group takes its mission very seriously.

The Glovers' website welcomes us into their realm, governed by the "Master of the Court," who rules with a retinue of "Under Wardens." Ann Esslemont, the Master as of this writing, wears a serious expression with her flowing ceremonial robe and elbow-length gauntlet gloves embroidered with an official-looking crest.

The Company's enormous collection encompasses "heritage items" from the 16th and 17th century including coronation gloves. When you enter the exalted and rarified world of the titled, you recognize that a glove is not a glove is not a glove but the embodiment of that society's mores and customs. During a coronation ceremony for the British monarchy, the sovereign's right-hand glove is removed so that a coronation ring can be slipped on. But if a member of royalty or the gentry is disgraced, he is stripped of his gloves. So that fine kidskin carries a lot of weight.

Not all gloves in the Company's collection are so imposing. Among the contemporary items are gloves of eye-popping orange that could have been worn in London's Swinging Sixties, along with one of only three 21st century examples: black gloves rescued from dullness by multi-colored polka dots, pink-tipped fingers and matching ostrich trim around the wrists. Website copy describes them as "A pair of ladies' black gloves of the early 21st Century, made in England . . . out and out fun gloves, suitable for parties, which show what can be done with imagination."

In its mission to promote glove knowledge to today's public (which includes bare-handed men and women who prefer to slouch about in cold weather with unbuttoned coats for that insouciant look), I wonder if the Glovers' work has become more difficult. I am gearing up the courage to email the question to the Master of the Court, and fantasize a lively exchange. In the old days, they played a vital role, forbidding the sale of gloves in candlelight because buyers might be unable to distinguish between properly made gloves and those of shoddy quality ("haughtie and deceitfulle gloves"). And so the Worshipful Company probably acted as a kind of early Consumer Protection Bureau. For that alone, the British public should be grateful.

My attempt to justify my passion for "clothing for the hands" through historical research has led to some interesting revelations. The ancient Romans wore gloves although Musonius, a philosopher, grumbled, "It is shameful that persons in perfect health should clothe their hands and feet with soft and hairy coverings." Musonius who? Mainly ignored, he's been consigned to obscurity. Practical Romans knew better, donning gloves both soft and hairy to survive winter in the Alps and the more intemperate regions of their far-flung empire. Maybe some Roman *fashionista* even decorated their gloves with jangling silver denarii, or the embroidered names of their favorite gladiators.

The gloves my mother stuffed my fingers into were neither soft nor hairy, but scratchy wool. As a child, I could not leave home without all digits covered, the edges of my gloves tucked tightly under my coat sleeves so that a quarter inch of wrist might not be exposed to the extremes of a New York City winter. At some point, the wool gave way to white cotton, pearl-buttoned gloves and later, kidskin. (I skipped gloves of chicken skin, all the rage among fashionable 16th century women, who wore the super-thin coverings at night to keep their hands soft.)

By the time I was a preteen, I was subscribing to *Glamour* and *Mademoiselle* and paying inordinate attention to every item of clothing that I wore. My well-dressed mother, a fashion oracle, proclaimed more than once, "You don't notice that a woman is wearing an inexpensive dress if she has high-quality accessories." Men were beginning to abandon their fedoras, but well-bred women were still required to cover their hands in public into the 1950s.

"... If beauty comes/it comes startled, hiding scars,/out of what barely can be endured," wrote poet Stephen Dunn in "Rubbing." Of course, as an item of clothing, gloves can hide physical imperfections. Chapped skin, bulbous knuckles, birthmarks or the coarsening that comes from physical labor—all could vanish, thanks to an attractive or even humble cover-up. It wouldn't be until the late sixties that divergence from the ideal was considered the charming enhancement of an individual's unique beauty, such as model Lauren Hutton's famous gapped teeth.

Of course, women were abandoning their cover-ups then, defying social mores by jettisoning gloves, bras, pantyhose, you name it. But I held fast. I wouldn't give up the gloves. I couldn't imagine living without this mask that, ironically, could make a statement about who I was or at least aspired to be. I envisioned someone smart, creative, even avant-garde and found myself saving up from summer jobs for the unusual (read, "expensive") gloves that would communicate these qualities.

No more basic black for me, except for funerals and job interviews in winter. Bring on purple, bottle green, hot pink, red. Bring on gauntlet gloves like those worn by knights who carried their ladies' perfumed gloves in their helmets as they galloped into battle. Bring on gloves with mathematical symbols, gloves stitched with hearts and spades—all handmade in Italy, where locals know the importance of presenting oneself in the best possible light (*fare una bella figura*).

As an assistant editor of an Italian American magazine, I was once inspired to read the first-person account of a jobless woman in a new city who was down to her last $50--and spent it all on a pair of hand-sewn *guanti* from Naples, considering them an investment in what truly mattered. I remember that the gloves were ecru, a very impractical color. She was my hero.

Inevitably, in 2007, I lost one of my treasures, a scarlet glove with prominent stitching and a saucy black arrow pointing towards the wrist ("Follow the arrow to the pulse of this vivacious person," I hoped it signaled). These gloves had been my biggest splurge to date, a birthday gift to myself. I went into mourning for the missing mate as I gazed forlornly at the glove left behind whose public life had ended. Briefly I thought of the mad scientist in *Dr. Strangelove* who wore a black glove on his out-of-control artificial hand. One red glove might begin a new trend—but then I decided otherwise.

I knew that I couldn't part with it but neither could I bear the constant reminder of its loss, probably due to my own carelessness.

Every time I opened the bureau drawer, I'd wonder about the orphan alone on a city sidewalk or subway platform or trapped in a revolving door. So I did the next best thing: I bequeathed my glove to B. Amore, a sculptor and multimedia artist who has incorporated gloves into her work. Most of the gloves that appear in Amore's art are the worn cloth or leather gloves of laborers—given to her or found on the street—but through bronze-impregnated resin, they are transfigured.

Amore suggested that I write a poem and that we make a small "shrine" of the glove by placing it in a deep, ornate frame, with my poem as a backdrop. I loved the idea, but couldn't settle on the words. I kept envisioning Jenny Holzer-type truisms such as "When I lost my glove, I saw the handwriting on the wall" or "To lose the perfect mate wrenches my heart." I picture those lines on one of the long subway tunnels in Grand Central or Times Square but after all these years, they've remained only ideas.

Every glove is altered by the particular characteristics of the hand that filled its space, and by time and use, Amore says. I've suspected for some time that gloves have a secret life apart from the human who gives it warmth and shape. Once in winter, having placed my gloves on a diner counter while I waited for coffee, I sat transfixed, watching my empty glove mimic my living body. It lay sideways, black leather puckered over the missing ridge of knuckles, fingers curled palmward as if they could not, or would not, unclench. I gripped the steaming coffee in both hands and stared as the fingers slowly straightened, then tipped back to lie flat and still. It seemed that the gloves' fingers moved by their own volition—like the mouth of a ventriloquist's dummy that speaks without the ventriloquist (surely the most terrifying *Twilight Zone* episode is the one in which a malevolent dummy takes control of his master).

That feeling of something askew was in play when I prevailed upon my husband to drive with me to explore Gloversville. I had just come across an amazing cache of gloves in Saratoga Springs, in a down-market store hidden in a windowless mall. They appeared to be the mint-condition, unsold stock of a 1960s manufacturer. I was elated by this mother lode of acid green, Day-Glo lemon and fuchsia polyester gloves, some trimmed at the wrist with tiny brass chains. To this day, I sometimes revel in wearing them, a "bad taste" counterpoint to staid elegance.

Surely this miraculous discovery was a sign that the fates wanted me to visit Gloversville, only 30 miles from Saratoga. Even without falling into that glove collector's dream cache ($20 for the lot, by the way), I wouldn't have been able to resist the lure of what had been the center of America's glove making industry, once the humming home of over 200 manufacturers. According to town history, its lush hemlock forests provided ample bark needed for tanning, and leather production began there as early as the 18th century. From 1890 to 1950, 90 percent of all gloves sold in the U.S. traced their origins to that place.

Such facts in a New York State brochure pulled me north the way a five-star luxury resort with a spa and infinity pool might lure another tourist. Besides, the brochure tantalized with its fleeting mention of a glove museum that supposedly displayed gloves worn by the first astronauts, along with Michael Jackson's jeweled glove (later selling for $350,000 at auction). Oddly, there was no mention of the museum's address.

It was a hot Sunday afternoon when my husband and I rolled into Gloversville which, we thought at first, might account for the deserted streets. Where was everyone? The residential area was lined with old houses but not one soul was out washing a car, mowing a lawn, flipping hamburgers, walking a dog or even relaxing on a porch. Very eerie. Downtown was the same, except for a middle-aged man ambling past closed stores rather aimlessly. Having begun to wonder what dimension we had crossed into, we were relieved to catch sight of a fellow human being.

Pulling up slowly and rolling down my passenger's window, I asked in my chirpiest visitor's voice, "Can you please tell us where the Glove Museum is?" "Never heard of it," he muttered without a second's pause, and that was that.

I've learned that one man is attempting to preserve the town's history—a self-taught glove maker named Daniel Storto, born in Toronto into a family of immigrant Italian tailors. Storto, a fashion designer who once lived in Hollywood, has established himself in Gloversville where he uses tools from the 1800s passed on to him by the town's long-retired artisans. Called the "haute couturier of gloves" by *Vogue* editor Hamish Bowles, Storto told a *New York Times* reporter in 2009: "I thought I was a glove maker, but I wasn't a glove maker at all until I met the old-timers. Until I came here, I had no idea what you could do with the craft." With big-name fashion designers as his clients, and samples of his work in the Metropolitan Museum of Art, Storto has found success in his own eccentric way. One glove maker doesn't constitute a revival, but still I greatly admire Storto for setting up shop in this nearly forgotten town of 16,000.

When I think about gloves I've loved and sometimes lost, it's their exquisiteness rather than their utility that moves me. Succumbing to a sale against my better judgment, I recently bought a pair designed with a special fabric on the tips of the index fingers so that the wearer could stay gloved in cold weather while tapping on a smart phone or tablet computer. They proved useless, and I berated myself for wasting money on what could have gone towards one of those special pairs I covet: gloves that are objects of beauty.

It's worth taking a stand for an eternal verity, isn't it? To feel unembarrassed admitting that when I learned the Worshipful Company of Glovers had posted photos and descriptions of its collection online, I nearly swooned. Now, that very word evokes Victorian women of many neuroses, given to frequent fainting. Dear reader, that's not me. I know I'm struggling to help you and myself understand what this glove fixation is all about.

Again and again, I return to beauty. As someone who appreciates artistry and workmanship that honors the most intricate details, and as someone who honors words, how could I not be impressed with this description of just one pair of gloves owned by the Worshipful Company:

A pair of leather gloves, probably circa 1650-70, of white kid dyed
mid brown, suede side up, with narrow stepped gauntlet of yellow linen
embroidered in raised silver gilt purl wire and couched threads with
stylised pomegranates, edged with scalloped band of bobbin lace tipped
with sequins, the seams delicately overstitched then turned right side
out, the stitches extending from the elongated fingers to form pointing,
31cm long.

Grateful to the Internet, I happily pored over gloves glittering
with gold embroidery, adorned with flossed silk birds perched on
branches, scrolled with tulips and carnations, beaded, appliqued,
jewel-encrusted, crocheted, lace-trimmed, displaying scenes in
miniature reminiscent of a medieval tapestry. I admired all of these,
as well as the simplest gloves clearly made of the softest kidskin
and accented only with exuberantly bold hand-stitching.

How to explain? Maybe I should stop trying and end with a
painting, *Man with a Glove*, by the Renaissance master Titian (ca.
1488–1576). The subject of this psychological portrait is a young
man dressed in the fine clothing of the Venetian aristocracy—he
wears a black jacket and pleated white shirt with ruffled cuffs, a
small medallion on a gold chain and a ring on long, slender fingers.
But there is nothing of the dandy about this poised young man,
perhaps 20, whose sensitive, melancholy eyes gaze off to the side
as if lost in thought. Against a nearly black background, his fine,
pale face and eyes can haunt. My own eyes are drawn down to
a point of lightness in the painting, gloves of supple tan leather.
His gloved left hand casually holds the other glove, wrinkled from
wear and perhaps ever-so-slightly smudged. The young man, who
has never been identified, is known to us by his gloves. Although
I see him briefly in repose, I just know that he's going places.

FOOD FOR SURVIVAL

When I think of that time, I think of my hunger—for a job, friends, a place in the world. I think of notebooks, pages now yellow, half-filled with the tentative scrawl of a writer unsure of her thoughts and if they were worth recording. I remember the daytime hours I lay in bed, trapped by my recurring dream of being pressed by a blanket made of steel. But I also recall the feasts I eventually cooked—sensuous banquets that satisfied my deepest yearnings for something physical to return me to my senses.

Just 23, I was unemployed, laid off not just from my first job, but after many months of unemployment, from my second one, too, because my beloved New York City was going bankrupt.

My husband and I had moved from Queens to the Bronx three years earlier when we had married—partly to put some distance between ourselves and our well-intentioned but over-involved parents, but mainly because the rents were cheap. We joked that we finally lived in the only borough of the city located on the United States mainland. Although I was now connected by landmass to a few hundred million people, I felt for the first time in my life like an abandoned island. And that island was adrift.

Being unemployed, I spent what seemed like endless hours, weeks, months, in a place hostile at worst, and at best, indifferent to my plight. Most of my friends had scattered, some off to graduate school, others gainfully employed. Our new neighborhood didn't seem to have any other young couples living there—just a few families and a large population of seniors who spoke languages we didn't understand. I was like the protagonist in *Stranger in a Strange Land*, the best-seller of that era. My husband was not unsympathetic but at 26, he spent his days teaching physics to high school students who had no particular interest in the law of falling bodies and his nights wedging in graduate classes.

When I left the gloom of our ground-floor apartment, I felt as if I were stepping into a black-and-white movie. The people who passed me in the lobby and on the sidewalk were characters whose stories I'd never know. I remember them gliding past me like ghosts or moving in fits and starts like figures in an early newsreel shown in an old theater—the kind with velvet seats worn thin, and stars on the ceiling that have nearly faded out.

I moved through our four rooms like a sleepwalker. One day (or night—who could tell?), while my fingers ran aimlessly over the spines of books, they seemed to remember through their pores the touch of one in particular—my first cookbook. My best friend's mother had given me this gift when I was five years old and she had begun treating us to weekly Swedish cooking lessons. Its surface was slightly prickly, like gooseflesh, as if the book, recalling an earlier life in warm kitchens, could not adapt to the spiritual frisson of its new environment. I pulled it down—splattered, taped, its loose white pages falling at my feet like manna, a sustenance I didn't realize until then that I had been desperately hungering for.

I sat down on the rug, my heart leaping. Aromas seemed to rise from the pages. Once again, I tasted Swedish pancakes, small and golden like coins of the realm, topped with deep-ruby lingonberries and drizzled with honey from Uncle Eric's farm. I tasted buttery spritz cookies, whose dough we pressed through a star on a metal disc, and tiny meatballs made with freshly grated nutmeg, lolling in a bath of cream.

Learning how to make such luscious dishes was an entirely new experience because my mother, the only American-born child in a large, immigrant Sicilian family, believed that cooking should take no longer than the time required to heat a can of string beans or dissolve Jell-O granules in water. I knew from early exposure to my aunts' feasts that my brother and I were missing a fundamental right of life bestowed by our Italian heritage, a right that my cousins took for granted. And so for me, cooking became a joyful and sometimes stubborn rebellion against the first-generation American who herself rebelled against what she perceived as needless, Old World-imposed drudgery.

With that cookbook a catalyst for memory, I was feeling a primal pull, the human animal's need to be nurtured and to nurture. If I couldn't find a job now, at least I could create dishes that would provide immediate gratification for me and those I loved—dishes beautiful as art, but satisfying in a different way. A poem that never left my notebook reveals my state of mind:

THE HIGHER ART

Books crowd my life, my rooms,
stiff-spined and above reproach
like dowagers, proud and marooned.
But sometimes words choke me.
It's then I turn to Escoffier,
measuring egg yolks for soufflé,
concocting a consommé
or other creation, once consumed,
that leaves nothing for posterity.

If I were to rewrite that poem today, I'd cite Lydia Bastianich as my idol, but she had yet to come into popular awareness. For anyone with serious culinary aspirations then, Julia Child and her *Mastering the Art of French Cooking* were all that mattered.

From that point on, I immersed myself in this higher art. Now my days had a greater purpose that shielded me from the potentially crushing disappointments I'd later experience, such as being named a finalist for a dream job, but not getting it. How could I let that bother me?

A great part of my pleasure came from sharing my creations with others, beginning with my husband. "Cooking Italian" was in my very marrow from my earliest days of self-preservation in my mother's sterile kitchen. But during this period of gnawing fear—will the city ever recover? Will I ever find a job?—I needed to strike out on my own, exploring new tastes and terrains. Traveling

from vichyssoise to moussaka, from goulash to Galician garlic
soup, I roamed the culinary map, relishing the new lands that I
entered. On one salary—a teacher's, at that—I knew we couldn't
afford everything I wanted to cook, but there were enough new
dishes in the world waiting for me before I approached asparagus
tips topped with truffles.

As I gained confidence, I found myself contacting friends
I hadn't seen for a long time, hosting dinner parties for six and
gradually expanding to buffets for 20 third-cousins twice removed.
(The stars of these mega dinners were the always-affordable pasta
dishes.) Our four rooms seemed to expand, easily accommodating
the crowd. I was no longer embarrassed by my lack of employment because, as far as I was concerned, I was fully engaged in
very valuable work. In fact, the fruits of my labor were much in
demand.

Relatives bought me coffee-table cookbooks that were my
passport to Italy. I spent hours in the as-yet-unvisited homeland
of the grandparents I never knew, gazing upon ancient olive trees
wrapped tenderly in white cloaks at harvest time like revered
elders. Handmade *orchiette, fettucine, farfalle* and countless other
poetically named pasta shapes were photographed on tables set
amid rolling Umbrian hills or on Palermo terraces flanked by
16th-century churches. No longer holed up in a $150-a-month
Bronx apartment that stole two hours of light a day, I was strolling
my ancestors' sunny, almond-perfumed hills, resolving to travel
there when the paychecks resumed. Not many years later, I did,
scribbling notes on every meal.

When the time was right, we invited both sets of parents for
dinner. Only years later, knowing their preference for the simplest,
blandest food, did I realize their tremendous self-restraint during
the all-Indian dinner we served with great pride. The adventure
began with Mulligatawny soup, moved on to chicken vindaloo
with pistachio-studded saffron rice pilaf and *raita* (cucumbers in
yogurt), and ended with *firni*—rice pudding flavored with rose
water, which I think of as a kind of edible perfume.

Tracking down the elusive rose water ingredient over the course of several weeks brought me out of my Bronx neighborhood into unfamiliar communities and grocery stores stocked with exotic foods and pungent spices. But instead of feeling like a stranger in a strange land, I was an explorer like Marco Polo, discovering pasta in China.

Throughout this time, I'd continued my job hunting and found one by pure serendipity. Noticing that the weekly community newspaper was published two blocks from our apartment, I stopped in to introduce myself and learned that the only reporter had just jumped ship. I was hired on the spot. The job was part time and paid only $100 a week, but it changed everything. Through interviews, I got to know neighbors, local elected officials and merchants, including a new, beleaguered fruit-and-vegetable vendor—probably one of New York's first from Korea—whose remark I quoted in my article: "If you're Italian, they think you're in the Mafia. If you're Korean, that means you're a Moonie."

Not everyone was a ghost after all.

I kept on cooking.

A random news release I received at the paper announced the launch of a new monthly magazine "celebrating all things Italian—its culture and countryside, fashions, art, design, and food." Seeing the last word, I read no further. I was ecstatic when I was called for an interview, landed a position as assistant editor and began working in a Manhattan high-rise just around the corner from Fifth Avenue.

I needn't have given a thought to fitting in. My first day on the job, I learned that the office had a full-size kitchen and co-workers just as crazy about cooking as I was. We all wanted to edit the food articles and review the newest Italian restaurants, so we democratically took turns.

And sometimes, in this pre-microwave era, we served one another lunch—elaborate, multi-course banquets suitable for the Medicis, each dish carefully carried on the subway into Manhattan from our far-flung neighborhoods in "the outer boroughs." I told my story of giving up my seat on the crowded train to the lasagna Bolognese and, watching my colleagues erupt into knowing laughter, I couldn't believe my good fortune. We traded recipes, fought, shared stories, ate in one another's homes, became a family.

My career in paradise ended after 14 months when the magazine folded for lack of advertising. My successful cooking at home had saved me from despair, that voracious wolf. But I'd moved beyond food for survival. Ironically, I'd tasted *la dolce vita* in a place quietly going bankrupt—even so, decades later, that rich flavor lingers.

MY LOST KINGDOM

On lunch breaks, escaping my gray government desk, I'd wander the aisles of a kingdom floating a few steps above street level in a 19th-century building. It was a domain of great calm and beauty filled not with gold and jewels, but shoes the colors of wildflowers. Agreed, a shoe is not a shoe is not a shoe, and doctoral theses have been written on the subject from the perspective of sociology, history, anthropology and, above all, contemporary culture—especially after *Sex and the City* made Manolo Blahniks and Jimmy Choos fetish objects for a certain kind of aspiring urbanite. My awareness of all that came later and had no bearing on me. I was only 22, not Cinderella trying on her missing slipper, and I wasn't prone to analyzing why I gravitated to the kingdom, a cavernous store called Anbar's Shoes. I just knew that it was a refuge for me.

My soul-deadening office job at a city agency during New York's 1970s downturn was only temporary, I believed, because I was destined for a satisfying career elsewhere—a sure-footed executive editor (a democratic mentor-type, of course), wearing what I just might discover in the next hour. The floorboards dated to the Industrial Era of this former factory, windows filtered wan light from twelve feet above, dust motes moved lazily in the air, but no matter. Atop each neat stack of boxes, one sample was posed, toe turned outward, ready to be filled and then to flee the dreariness that awaited me after the magic hour had ended. Those shoes were made for dancing into my future.

I'd learned about this self-service store from a co-worker. Before I ever heard of Philippine First Lady Imelda Marcos and her 3,000 pairs of shoes, there was Sally, a hard-working civil servant who had been treating herself to a new pair with each biweekly paycheck. This had been going on for years before I arrived, desperate for a job after college, and so it was rare for me to see Sally wearing the same shoes twice. As her fleet fingers typed unending bureaucratic reports, underneath the grim metal desk her purple platform shoes tapped to a different beat. One visit to the store and I was hooked.

Now, so many years and shoes later, I stop and ask myself why the store was not a store but a kingdom to me. The shoes' effect was transporting—a reaction that to my adult self at first might seem over the top, even for a very young woman. That is, until I did some research and came across a 2015 BBC culture feature, *Ten Shoes That Changed the World*. Seeing those inflated words, which I half-expected to carry the subtitle "The Power and the Glory," made me think that as a devoted subject in the Kingdom of Shoes, I was actually a paragon of maturity and modulation.

It turns out that footwear fascination—o.k., obsession—has been around for millennia. The chattering classes have called shoes "cultural signifiers," objects that speak volumes about their wearers and their society. Of course, they're status symbols, too, beginning with sandals embellished with pure gold leaf and shaped nothing like the human foot—sound familiar? —worn by Roman fashionistas (30 BC-300 AD). The fact that they may also inflict torture on the wearer is beside the point.

Just about any shoe style we think is modern is not. Platform shoes worn by glam rockers, not to mention Vivienne Westwood's eight-inchers that sent Naomi Campbell tumbling on the catwalk? An old concept recycled through the ages. High-class courtesans in feudal Japan wore a lacquered version called "getas" that were the same insane height—forcing them to walk very slowly for better viewing by males. In ancient Greece, actors who wanted the advantage of standing out on a crowded stage donned platform shoes. And in the 14th century Ottoman Empire, clogs elevated bathers' feet over scummy, slippery floors. Last year, London's Victoria and Albert Museum curated an exhibit, "Shoes: Pleasure and Pain." Among the 200 pairs of shoes on view were mother-of-pearl Turkish bath clogs towering nearly a foot high.

After viewing the exhibition, reporter Kathryn Hughes wrote in *The Guardian*: "Shoes matter . . . because they mark the place where our bodies contact the world and stories begin." This strikes me as a brilliant observation.

My story was just beginning that year of my first full-time job. In the middle of what felt like a Depression in my beloved city, fashion was an explosion of saturated colors—hot pink, lemon yellow, turquoise, violet. Browsing the store, stocked with scores of European imports, I could have been strolling through an Italian garden or Spanish sunflower field. Despite their pedigree, the shoes were deeply discounted, and in my cloak-and-dagger fantasy, kidnapped from plush-carpeted salons where elegant Old World salesmen knelt at the feet of rich women. Safely sequestered on a nondescript, even seedy side street downtown, they had found a better home where they would be appreciated by women with flat wallets but fine taste.

I would stroke the buttery leather, admire the creativity and craftsmanship of unique appliqué or an enameled buckle, and practice a confident strut before a wavy mirror. Once when I returned the beyond-my-budget objects of desire to their stack, sighing audibly, the silver-haired owner propositioned me. I can't recall the words, but I got the drift: for my favors, I could choose whatever shoes I wanted, whenever I wanted. He was whispering in my ear, spreading the riches of the Kingdom of Shoes before me. I stuttered "No, thank you" politely, before bolting.

My favorite purchase had a mythic, Proustian impact on me—proper navy blue pumps from Italy, but hand-painted with a dense, pink paisley pattern. They walked a fine line, the attempted balancing act of a person still in formation: admit into my life the classic influence of past times but subvert every inch with a quirky spirit. I wore those shoes more than a decade. Giving them up felt like losing part of myself.

I'm surprised I wrote that last sentence. But on reflection, not really, because shoes are so powerfully associated with personality. I think of my friend Christine. The first time I met her, she made an unforgettable impression in her knee-high gladiator sandals which, decades ago, were a rarity. I assumed she was an individualist, the kind of person who wasn't afraid to speak up for her beliefs. My

first impression, based on those "warrior" sandals, proved over time
to be right. And I think of my mother's sister, my Aunt Anna, who
advanced to become forelady at a prestigious menswear company
in the garment district and always dressed elegantly, head to toe.
We lived in the same two-family house and every morning as she
left, I heard the click-clack sound of her heels—they were always
pumps—against the pavement, loud at first and then fading as
she turned the corner. As *The Guardian* reporter might say, it was
the sound of a woman literally striking out—hitting the ground,
connecting with the world—in an era when few women were
employed outside the home. In my mind, my aunt's shoes were
part of her identity.

    And I think of my mother, ten years younger than Anna, and
her aura of glamour, of her pronouncements to me even as a child
about what well-dressed women should wear and avoid (red shoes
were the mark of a fallen woman; my black patent-leather Mary
Janes were just for summer wear). In my old files I find one of my
first post-adolescent poems:

MOTHER'S SHOES

Suede, patent, satin, kid and silk—
always at least 20 pairs
stacked neatly out of view
like piles of underwear.

I see her in matinal meditation
poised before the closet like Monet
before his palette, seeking the perfect shade.
She selects, wriggles into indigo
and clicks smartly up the sidewalk,
another Monroe.

Mother's shoes came and went.
In the 50s, spiked heels, lethal toes,
then it's chic to be sensible

and the swift, sure, reversal:
ballet flats, stacked heels, square toes.
Styles adopted, styles rejected:
vinyl boots, ankle straps,
earth shoes, rubber soles.

Lesson I: Wear a good pair of shoes
    and you'll look like a million.

Lesson II: Tactful women, like leather shoes,
    always give a little.

Mother's shoes came and went,
came and went, nesting each night,
foundlings in rows.

 Going back even further into early childhood, I recall the happiness of playing dress up with my mother's hats, gloves, jewelry and scarves. But nothing connected me to her and to an adult future more strongly than slipping my little feet into her size 8 pumps. The loud clomping sound the shoes made as I paraded through the apartment was satisfying, as if to announce, "Here I am!" Although I was much too young to know that a deeper metaphor of filling another's shoes was at work, I seemed to sense the shoes' larger significance in a visceral way.

 Today you can't think about shoes as "cultural signifiers" without focusing on stilettos—named appropriately for a superthin, easily hidden dagger that can swiftly kill. Call them "needle heels" for the killer elite—those who can afford nearly a grand for a pair of Manolo Blahniks. Ever since 1955 when Christian Dior's designer Roger Vivier made a prototype strong enough to withstand the wearer's weight, the stiletto shoe has been equated with sex and power. I can't help picturing female assassins puncturing the ground as they stalk their prey, leaving behind tiny air holes for the damned below.

Certainly the signature red-soled stiletto by French designer Christian Louboutin (the best-selling model, Pigalle, named after the Paris red-light district) is a contemporary fetish object for millions. The agony of actually trying to walk in them any farther than from limo to restaurant takes its toll, though. And that has given rise in the past few years to an extreme procedure, Botox injections into the ball of the foot. This so-called "stiletto lift" is said to reduce pain, at least temporarily, by padding the foot with filler in the spot of greatest pressure. Some call it a "Loub job." According to Wednesday Martin's popular 2015 memoir, *Primates of Park Avenue*, the technique is in favor among privileged Upper East Side women who refuse to give up their killer heels. Their husbands are only too happy to provide financing.

One employee of a British surgery clinic told *The Sun*, "Loub job requests have now surpassed bookings for lip fillers. Women aged from 18 to 60 are asking for the procedure because all women want to wear beautiful shoes. If you think of the money they spend on shoes, having a Loub job is a sound investment."

And whenever there's a consumer need, someone will invent a new product to fill the gap. In 2013 Heel No Pain came on the market, giving stiletto addicts the less invasive option of trying a highly concentrated foot-numbing spray that contains an ingredient used by dentists. Whatever gets you through a night on the town.

But lately there have been some positive signs of rebellion against what, it seems to me, is the modern equivalent of whalebone corsets. I cheered Julia Roberts when I learned that she had suddenly cast off her stilettos on the Cannes Film Festival red carpet. The photo of her barefoot in an Armani gown went viral. Kristen Stewart did the same. The year before, a group of women in their 50s had been turned away for wearing flats, and actress Emily Blunt took the lead in protesting. She called a press conference and, referring to the high-heel dress requirement at Cannes, said, "That's very disappointing, just when you kind of think there are waves of equality."

Ah—there it is. A woman's right to refuse to wear the vamp/temptress uniform, to wear whatever she wants, whether it's athletic shoes, platforms, kitten heels, Mary Janes or loafers. Or the right to play the vamp if she chooses, but closer to the ground (easier to make a quick escape?). I can't help wondering if Audrey Hepburn would have been ejected from Cannes if she had shown up in her trademark ballet flats for opening night of *Funny Face*. Curiosity compels me to go searching, and bingo, I find a Cannes Festival photo of Hepburn in a white evening gown accessorized not with flats but the tiniest heels. Holding the opposite arm of her tuxedoed escort, an unidentified actress thrusts one sharp-toed stiletto.

A week earlier than the Julia Roberts episode, a temp receptionist in England named Nicola Thorp, 27, was receiving her own media attention for refusing to conform to "foot dress code." The ruckus began when she appeared in flats her first day on the job at a major financial corporation and was sent home without pay for not wearing two-to-four-inch heels. Thorp objected to the requirement, described her experience on Facebook and quickly heard from many sympathetic women. That led to her posting a Parliamentary petition stating, "Make it illegal for a company to require women to wear high heels at work." With 148,300 signatures at the time of this writing, she has catapulted over the 100,000 signature minimum that, in England, automatically guarantees a Parliamentary debate on the issue. Does the House of Commons have C-Span? That is one debate I'd like to hear.

Within my Lost Kingdom, I never thought about feminism and its relationship to shoes, although I was a budding feminist. I never sought any particular status brand. I didn't care if the shoes I might discover had flat, mid or high heels, only that they be exquisitely made. What I really craved and needed at that stressful time of my life were objects of beauty. I also felt a visceral hunter's thrill, never knowing what I would find. But none of this adequately explains why I was drawn there and why I still remember my visits so vividly.

I realize now that my deep pleasure was mostly about the experience—when I was inside the store, I felt that I existed, at least for a while, in a predictable, orderly environment that was becoming hard to find elsewhere. My frustration at work had been growing. Spending stultifying hours writing job descriptions for the Department of Social Services in a bleak office was not the career I had envisioned after the pleasures of Shakespeare and T.S. Eliot. Just riding to work every day inside ugly subway cars hastily covered with spray paint or black marker was to feel trapped in a netherworld's maze where anything could, and did, happen. On top of that, the unrelenting news of my city's bankruptcy, layoffs, and increasing street crime was deeply unsettling.

By contrast, I felt peaceful and at ease in this beautiful kingdom. I had the feeling that it was run by people behind the scenes who cared for its happy subjects—people ruled by logic, aesthetics, even scientific principles. Thousands of shoes were color-coded and precisely arranged according to the spectrum: red, orange, yellow, green, blue, indigo and violet. Chartreuse could be found exactly where it belonged, in between yellow and green; teal shoes positioned between green and blue. I pictured a color chart on the stockroom walls being consulted like a chemist's Table of the Elements. The world might be coming apart outside, but here, all was carefully inspected, checked off and accounted for. Ultimately, I believe that's why it felt to me like a haven.

I've since learned the futility of expecting order and certainty in the world or my life. Ambiguity, doubt, confusion, even, at times, chaos—that's what I count on. Although the kingdom is lost—replaced by a bank surrounded by multimillion-dollar con- dos—I still recall the firm steps I took with such anticipation each time I crossed the threshold into that enchanted realm. I did not plod there, head down. I did not totter. For one hour, I soared.

III. The Italian Thing

SICILY: MY ENIGMA

I could begin this journey on black pavement of volcanic lava, destruction/construction as Sicilian metaphor embodied in a town whose name I don't recall. Or nearly knocked backwards by the sight of Greek temples shining in spring sun on a poppy-studded hillside, a seeming mirage too magnificent to be real. In Sicily it's easy to succumb to the intoxication of jasmine and honeysuckle, to enter a garden and feel yourself spinning dizzily within galaxies of lemon trees.

Or I can begin on a drive through the nearly deserted streets of Lercara Friddi, past my great-grandmother's crumbling house and stores with dusty shelves in this once-prosperous sulphur mining town that my grandfather fled over a century ago. My young, distant cousin Salvatore is at the wheel, and although I need a bilingual speaker to interpret his words, I can sense shyness in his bearing and lowered eyes. "Is the Mafia here?" my traveling companion Marie asks him. Salvatore rolls the car windows all the way up and glances nervously over his shoulder before answering, *È a tutti banni* ("It's everywhere" in Sicilian). Fifteen miles from Corleone and 12 from Prizzi, we're in the black heart of it.

Or how about cruising with the glitterati in Taormina in your Dolce & Gabbana silk sheath accessorized with "pumps in Taormina lace with crystals" ($995) and a "clutch in brocade with jeweled daisies" ($3,595)—flashing your Euros and chic taste in the shadow of Etna, that heaving fire-breather just waiting for a chance to bury you. In Sicily the dead are also everywhere: in roadside memorials for the crime-fighting judges Falcone and Borsellino. In the bells that small towns toll early mornings when a resident passes away during the night: three for men, four for women. In the sudden appearance of street corner niches that shelter photographs of the departed. Oh Sicily! The Mafia. The beauty. The dead.

But for now I'll begin at a white enamel table in the scrubbed kitchen of an apartment on 103rd Street in East Harlem, an early 20th century Italian immigrant enclave. My Sicilian grandmother Nunzia—black-clad, aproned, tiny, her yellow-gray hair pulled into a bun—is not a stereotype to me because at age eight, I know nothing about Sicily or Italy or ingrained concepts of their people. I have no idea of who she is, this old lady who jabbers in a strange language and always tries to press a dollar bill into my hand while my mother jabbers back some kind of unsuccessful protest.

In our weekly visits to Manhattan from Queens, I'm crossing not the East River but an ocean into a foreign country. Mysterious the hallway and narrow, creaking steps in the four-story tenement building that my grandfather Domenico managed to buy, his business acumen part of the family lore. Mysterious my grandfather in the group portrait—stocky, mustached, with deep-set, determined black eyes watching from the bedroom bureau, surrounded by votive candles flickering before holy cards and statues of the Sacred Heart, the Virgin Mary, St. Anthony and St. Anne. What did I know of him, either, dead before I was born?

Moving through the interior, windowless rooms of that railroad flat is like passing through a series of sacred chambers in a primordial cave. I feel the intimate hush of small spaces mixed with a sense of timelessness. During my passage, I wonder which room was the one where my mother was born, the baby of the family and the only American native among five children.

My mother, Concetta ("Connie"), was the la'Americana with a vengeance, hating to cook, serving me and Bob anything and everything that was canned, dried, frozen, instant or powdered. (My father, also a first-generation American, traced his family to the Campania region; orphaned at a young age and raised by nuns, he relished any food put before him, even canned fruit cocktail.) My mother rejected traditional Old World customs such as wearing black in extended mourning and laying flowers at the graves of deceased family members. "Visit me when I'm alive—that's what counts," she always said and still does now.

And yet Bob and I absorbed a Sicilian sensibility because the island's influence on my transplanted grandparents and therefore on my mother was so powerful. Even before her birth, Sicily had seeped into her genetic code. And so, she is scrupulously clean; suspicious of strangers despite an appearance of friendliness; fatalistic; an interpreter of usually foreboding dreams; and frugal yet fond of collecting jewelry and clothing befitting a contessa and surrounding herself with antiques that could have furnished a palace in the Kingdom of the Two Sicilies. She is also deeply religious. The same saints keep vigil on her dresser just as they did in my grandmother's apartment, but Padre Pio and Saint Jude have joined the group, lit with an electric candle. My mother is, in short, a mass of contradictions that, I suspect, may be true of every first-generation American.

For our own amusement, as teenagers Bob and I compiled a homemade mini-book, *The World According to Concetta: Sayings of a Sicilian American Mother*. Chapter One, "On Dealing With the Outside World," began with "Don't trust anyone" and went on to "Never tell anyone your business." I hear those words as I tell this story, aware that I'm breaking the rules with every sentence. The silence of law-abiding families like ours, I believe, related to deep suspicion of "outsiders," and perhaps a feeling of ethnic inferiority in what was then a culture dominated by an Anglo Saxon ideal. We were also warned, "Don't get too friendly with anyone," "You've got to speak up or people will take advantage," "Don't carry your wallet in your back pocket," and "Make them put it in writing." Other chapters covered "Domestic Matters," "Keeping Up Appearances," "Staying Healthy," and ended with "Concetta, Sage and Prophet": "God is going to punish you," "There's a lot of evil in this world," "Mark my words," "It's all in the stars," and "I'm going to die young of a cerebral hemorrhage." At 93, my mother gets a failing grade as a sibyl.

Despite our fun at her expense which my mother, to her credit, accepted with good humor, we recognized that her view of life was essentially dark. Connie knew nothing about the history of Sicily's subjugation by one foreign occupier after another—Arabs, Greeks, Romans, Spaniards, Normans—the common explanation for such a distrusting world view. Yet there it was. When my mother smoked a borrowed cigarette at a wedding—an outrageous act of defiance that I realized, even as a girl, was done to scandalize our Sicilian relatives—it was insignificant compared to the island's power over her. She may have tried to be a truly modern American, but the New World lost the battle.

By the time we wrote *The World According to Concetta*, Bob and I had more than an inkling of what our Sicilian heritage meant: suspicion and fear of the "other," fierce self-reliance, and no sense of civic life or the commonweal, the latter summarized in the all-encompassing "Don't get involved." Signs and portents were also a natural part of life. If my mother was lecturing us and a church bell happened to ring, or something as small as a spoon clattered to the floor, she would utter, "See! It's true!" as if the spirits were signaling their agreement. Her dreams were always vivid, filled with visits from the dead.

*

When I was 11 years old, my concept of "Sicilianness" was forever changed by exposure to the real thing: the arrival of Tina, *una cugina* from Lercara Friddi whose name I'd never heard. Tina had written to my Aunt Anna, my mother's oldest sister, about her wish to emigrate, and my aunt and uncle agreed to take her in despite their cramped apartment in Queens. They did this despite the fact that Aunt Anna, who came to New York through Ellis Island as a nine-year-old, had never returned to Sicily to meet any of the current relatives whom we referred to collectively as "the Sicilians." My aunt found Tina a job in the garment district factory where Anna was forelady for a manufacturer of men's high-end suits. As a Sicilian-born female of a certain era, Tina had learned to sew expertly right out of the cradle, just like Aunt Anna.

Tina fascinated me. Her curly hair, unstylish dress, and lack of makeup were foreign, even exotic to my young eyes. Only in her late twenties, Tina seemed so much older. Yet she spoke as fast, if not faster than a native New Yorker, and I enjoyed the experience of hearing my mother and aunt try to keep up the conversation with a linguistically facile native in that chopped, almost guttural language.

I knew little or nothing about my grandmother or grandfather. And now, adding to the mystery was this blank-slate relative who may as well have dropped into our lives from another planet.

I wondered if the family had even known that Tina existed.

"Yes, over the years my mother did keep in contact with the Sicilians," my cousin Richard, Aunt Anna's younger son, told me. "When we were still living in East Harlem, she would send packages of food and clothing. I can picture her bundling the contents inside big white sheets that she stitched closed along the seams and then sealed with wax."

A few years ago, Tina's sister Josie revealed that my own toddler outfits had a second life in Sicily. Then I learned that before Tina arrived on the scene, Aunt Anna was startled one day to receive photos of a Sicilian celebration held in honor of Richard's recent marriage. Tables had been set up in a Lercara Friddi piazza, a meal was served, and wedding favors distributed that were embossed with the names of bride and groom. Between this incident and the knowledge that "the Sicilians" were going about their lives wearing our clothes, I had the feeling that Lercara Friddi was a kind of parallel universe to ours.

In that isolated mountain town, women were expected to live, marry and die in the place where God had chosen them to be born. In this context, I now realize how spunky Tina had been to strike out. In New York, it wasn't long before Tina had saved enough money to help bring over her parents, her younger sister Josie, and her brother Joe. Each one in turn returned to Lercara to marry locals (naturally)—all of their spouses eager to leave Sicily behind. They found jobs, had children, bought houses in the suburbs, and their children became educated, successful professionals. You know the story, repeated by millions of other hard-working immigrant families.

But let's face it: immigrant stories are never simple, with no loose ends and everything neatly tied up in a red-white-and-blue bow. This is a Sicilian American story: there are knots and frays, a ribbon twisting on itself like a Möbius strip.

In 1983 as an editor at the Italian American magazine *Attenzione*, I was incredibly fortunate to visit Italy on assignment. The trip, my first to my ancestral homeland, reverberated deeply for me and led to one of my first published poems, "Vesuvius," about a near-death experience in a tunnel near Naples. Subsequent trips to Italy inspired other poems set in Spaccanapoli, the oldest section of Naples, the Roman Forum, Pompeii, and in the courtyard of Verona's "House of Juliet." But visiting Sicily for the first and, so far, only time in 2007 unsettled me to the core, entangling me in a web of conflicting images and emotions that I kept grappling with and, until now, couldn't even attempt to express. No new poems came from that trip, just notebook jottings like hieroglyphs. Sipping fresh-squeezed blood orange juice at breakfast on a cliff-side terrace overlooking the sea and an active volcano was to watch myself as if I were a character in a play. I was in Sicily at last, but couldn't shake the feeling of unreality, of floating above myself.

Things became even more surreal when I took the bus heading southeast from Palermo to Lercara Friddi, accompanied by Marie, my husband's Italian-speaking cousin. We drove out of the congested city, the clogged traffic giving way to gently rising hills. The old bus then chugged its way up a more vertical incline, reaching the town's bus depot less than an hour later. It was chilly there in the higher altitude, befitting the Friddi ("cold") in the town's name. (The first word, Lercara, is said to derive from the Arabic *al kara*, meaning "quarter.")

We were greeted by Angela, the daughter of Tina's brother Joe, who shocked the family many years earlier by uprooting his wife Enza and American-born children Angela, then 12, and Salvatore, five years old, from their home on Long Island and permanently moving back to Lercara. Such reverse migrations don't fit the success stories we tell. No one could comprehend why Joe would do such a thing. Hearing the news, I'd shuddered for his family, devastated by his decision, suddenly thrown backwards in time and forced to live in a culture that couldn't be more different than late 20th century America's.

When I met Enza that day, I saw only deep sadness in her eyes. But to Marie, a complete stranger who struggled to understand the dialect, she was a Medea who poured out her rage, barely contained after more than a decade. "To bring me back here was bad enough," she lamented. "But to destroy my children's future—I will never forgive him!" It was only during the bus ride back to Palermo that I learned what had been said during their huddled conversation.

The apartment where we had gathered was dark and heavy, as if Enza's anger had seeped into the air. And so I welcomed the chance to escape when Angela offered to give us a tour that overcast April day, her brother Salvatore at the wheel. Using English recalled from childhood, Angela pointed out my grandmother's home and my great grandmother's clearly abandoned birthplace. I had to see the older house up close and left the car to climb the steeply pitched street.

We were a thousand metaphorical miles from Taormina's dazzle. Wires angled across the rough concrete façade, plywood covered a broken window and grass tufts sprouted through the stone blocks at its threshold. The town's 18th-century baroque cathedral, Santa Maria della Neve, was locked mid-day. Later I read that this church was where the infamous Salvatore Lucania ("Lucky" Luciano) was baptized and Frank Sinatra's grandfather Francesco was married. Orange plastic fencing separated the cathedral steps from a construction area, but no workers were in sight.

When my cousins took us to the lower part of Lercara Friddi, we were utterly alone. I wondered what they were thinking as I knelt before the remains of the sprawling, two-story railroad station that once served this town, called Little Palermo in its heyday. Was I praying for the people, past, present and future, of this forsaken place? Genuflecting before a building façade that still retained traces of classical beauty in its Corinthian columns and graceful pediments? Or was I simply on my knees to better photograph the field of lemon-yellow wildflowers and misty blue hills seen through its doorless openings, and the trees shouldering their way through the once-crowded waiting room? Nearby, a concrete silo and clay-tile-roofed buildings told the story of a farm that had harvested its last crop many decades ago.

Only walking in the hills with my cousins, breathing deeply and watching Angela's little girl Concettina pick herbs did my feeling of heaviness lift. In the town itself, I felt the burden of blocked-off mines and high unemployment, pavement in disrepair and, from the look of the few people we passed on the street, a broken spirit. They appeared beaten down, as if they expected nothing from life. The pall was almost palpable. Even the men in their tweed caps, smoking and playing cards in a patch of sun, had morose expressions.

While walking through the commercial area, I wondered why there were no sit-down restaurants.

"Anyone wanting to open a new business knows they'll get a slip of paper with an amount written on it," Salvatore explained. "So no one opens anything here. For pizza, we travel to another town."

And then I recalled Tina telling us that the Mafia even controlled the flow of water to the town faucets when she was growing up. I felt waves of anger and sadness, remembering Aunt Anna's late-in-life tale of why my grandfather, a proud, prosperous store-owner, left the town in 1907: he refused to be extorted. When three men "visited" his store to apply more pressure in the form of a pointed gun, my grandfather reached for the rifle he kept under his counter. Bullets flew and one hit a Mafioso, mortally wounding him. And so Domenico fled to America. More than 100 years later, seemingly nothing has changed there.

*

My mother's older brothers and sisters have passed away, and my first cousins who once lived as children in my grandparents' East Harlem building are now in their seventies. My brother spends hours on the Ellis Island website examining ship manifests, trying to piece together a coherent narrative that would explain my grandfather's several trips to New York following his first one in 1907. When did my grandmother come? And her brothers? And my aunts and uncles? Who was the person on Carmine Street in Little Italy they were visiting? And on Elizabeth Street? And Houston Street? And so I find myself turning to the Sicilian relatives here, the link to my family and the condemned, enchanted island that attracts, repels, excites, energizes and maddens me.

For a while, Tina and Josie had wanted to visit my mother, who has a lifelong aversion to traveling more than a few miles by car. And so a few months ago I invited them, their children and spouses to have lunch at my home with my mother as guest of honor. It was a crisp, sunny autumn day filled with much laughter and chatter in English and dialect among the generations, a day etched with unusual clarity in my memory.

At one point, while sitting at my table, Tina and Josie began to speak quietly to each other, their facial expressions thoughtful and concerned. Tina's daughter Bernadette interpreted: "They're trying to decide if they should tell your mother something. They don't want to upset her." After more deliberation, they went ahead, addressing my mother for several minutes as she listened intently.

"What was that all about?" I quickly asked Bernadette.

"They said that your family name was chosen. Your grandfather's father was a very wealthy married businessman in Lercara who had servants and got one of them pregnant. The baby—your grandfather—was turned over to the church, which found a poor couple to raise him. They received money for his care. But the couple didn't give him their family name. Instead they found a name that no one in the town had."

To me, this revelation, told to Tina and Josie's mother by a contemporary of my grandfather, was a bombshell. "It's bullshit," Bob instantly reacted when I repeated the story, also insisting that the Mafia confrontation tale defies credibility. My mother, paradoxically practical despite her superstitions, shrugged her shoulders when she heard the story behind her maiden name. "It doesn't matter to me," she said. "That was all so long ago."

What to believe? So hard to separate truth from half-truths and outright fabrications, especially when all the witnesses are long dead. Still, when my mother commented, "My father never mentioned anything about this," and Richard later added, "Come to think of it, I heard about grandma's past but nothing about grandpa's," the story began to have the ring of truth.

A few days later, unable to stop pondering, I emailed Bernadette. "Was your mother ever told the name of the rich man who was my grandfather's father? I would love to know!" She went back to her mother to ask but answered no, to my huge disappointment. Who was the blood of his blood? And why do I even care?

Maybe my mother is the true American, able to separate a given name from an identity, dismissing the past as irrelevant to her life—while I, the second-generation American, am drawn back, capable of falling under the spell of history's secrets.

A few weeks before I started to write this piece, I picked up *The Stone Boudoir: Travels Through the Hidden Villages of Sicily*, a memoir by the Sicilian American journalist Theresa Maggio. My husband had given me this book about a decade ago, knowing my keen interest in Sicily, but somehow I couldn't turn to it until now.

In one chapter, Maggio was investigating her family line in the town of Santa Margherita, home of the hundred-room palace where Giuseppe di Lampedusa, author of *The Leopard*, spent his summers in childhood. Later the palace was almost completely destroyed by earthquake.

Ironically, she wrote: "I had hoped to find in the birth records some hint that I could be the product of 'prima nox,' a baron's right to spend the first night with all the brides of his realm. If a woman protested that she was married, the baron might hang her husband and make her a widow."

But Maggio's ancestors were all legitimate. If not, she says, the birth records would have indicated that with the notation "Found on the wheel," a kind of revolving drawer at orphanages where children born out of wedlock were left anonymously. She writes (italics mine): "*For a surname, those babies were often given family names from out of town, according to the town clerk who helped me decipher the writing. An out-of-town name would mark the child for life, and make her suffer for the sin of her parents.*" More weight tipping the scales towards the truth of the tale that Tina and Josie told us, despite my brother's skepticism.

If my grandfather's reputed origins are true, was he looked down upon, even shunned, by the people of Lercara? According to my cousins, people knew at the time about Domenico's father and his unacknowledged son. But they claimed that my grandfather's success was viewed as evidence of his inherited business talent and his own determination, qualities that were called upon in America. Even having to start all over at the age of 28, he rose from a dangerous, back-breaking job as a subway sandhog to opening a neighborhood candy store, eventually purchasing the apartment building on 103rd Street where the family lived, and renting the next-door stables to a variety of pushcart owners.

"We had everything," my Aunt Anna said about her childhood in Lercara Friddi, the same words my mother used about her childhood in East Harlem, even during the Depression.

Yet I have so many questions. Who was my great grandmother? What happened to her after she gave birth and her son was taken away? Was she herself sent away from the villa where she had worked, forced into a life of shame and struggle? Did my grandfather know her name? Did he ever see her, talk to her, hold her?

Although I can't stop wondering about Domenico's real surname, I also realize that ultimately, it doesn't matter, that what counts is the man he was and what he accomplished. I've heard stories of his strength—how this burly man, five feet three inches tall, lifted a full wine barrel alone that two men couldn't budge. I've heard about his temper and stubbornness. And my mother's admission that he spoiled her terribly as the American baby, giving her everything she wanted. And also that he managed to hold on while suffering from heart disease, dying three days after he heard that my mother had delivered a healthy boy. Of course, these are second-hand stories, but they are all I have.

A *New York Times* review of *L'Attesa* ("The Wait"), set in Sicily around Easter time when I visited, reverberated for me. Writing about Piero Messina's debut feature loosely based on a Pirandello play, film critic A.O. Scott described the beauty of the landscape: "volcanic rock and quiet forests surrounding a sparkling lake . . . The setting has an atavistic, primal grandeur. Sicily is a place of ancient blood feuds, medieval rituals and Greek tragedies."

How can I not return, plunging into that labyrinth again, knowing I will find only more mysteries? How can I ignore the call, beyond all reason, of this island on my soul?

LIFE INSIDE MY NAME

September: first day of fourth grade class at St. Joan of Arc school. All 50 of us baby boomers are tightly packed into long rows, watching and listening with nervous anticipation as Sister Mary of the Rosary reads aloud each name on the class register with magisterial authority from her imposing desk. "Here!" One by one, each child responds, raising a hand. I'm near the end of the alphabet, so I have time to note who among these classmates I know and who is new to me.

Time's up—Sister has reached the R's. "AN-NA-MA-RI-A-RO-TON-DI," she pronounces loudly and slowly, drawing out the nearly perfect dactylic meter of my name. "It sounds just like a ship sailing up and down on the ocean." The class roars with laughter at her unexpected witticism, and I'm grateful that my face never reddens to reveal embarrassment. Instead I feel as if my blood is draining out, my body sinking into that ocean she's conjured up.

Only now I stop and wonder, which ship did I represent? No doubt, the Santa Maria, that sailing ship from the Old World, probably creaking and leaking as it was buffeted about. Surely not the Queen Elizabeth, the super-luxurious liner of the time, or a sleek, hundred-foot-long yacht cutting through the waves on its way to a glamorous island, chic passengers sunning themselves on deck.

When our teacher called the next name, the laughter subsided, but it took me beyond the letter Z to recover from my humiliation. What could I do about my name, a ridiculous total of eight, count them, eight vowel-laden syllables? My last name wasn't bad (although even then as an eight-year-old I was aware that "Rotondi" meant round and, by extension, fat). But at least it was only three syllables. Then why did my parents have to destroy that advantage by giving me the five-syllable first name Annamaria? As if they recognized that it would be a mouthful for others and a problem for me, they always called me Maria. In any formal setting, though, I'd cringe as my full name was invariably mangled when announced. If I gently corrected, I risked a frown that implied my identity was an impediment to the smooth functioning of the social order.

The unease I felt because of my long, very Italian-sounding name began in that fourth grade classroom. I longed to be the four-syllabled Cathy Murphy (and yes, I also wished I'd been born with her blonde hair and blue eyes). Or even better, Joan Smith, bland, swift at play in the schoolyard and popular as peanut butter on white bread. At that time, Maria was an exotic name that I shared with only one other classmate, a girl who recently fled with her family from Castro's Cuba. It was nothing like Mary or even Marie, those happy, pig-tailed rope-jumpers. In contrast, Maria, with her somewhat languid-sounding name, lay under a cloud of foreign influence—unfathomable, out of the mainstream, maybe not to be trusted.

Years later, I'd fall in love with the music of *West Side Story*, taking pride in the lush, gorgeous lyrics of the Steven Sondheim hit song, "Maria."

"Maria.
The most beautiful sound I ever heard:
Maria, Maria, Maria, Maria . . .
All the beautiful sounds of the world in a single word . . .
Maria! Say it loud and there's music playing.
Say it soft and it's almost like praying."

At last, recognition that my ethnic name was worthy of admiration. Vindication! Maybe the tide had turned.

Ironically, that very song opens the insightful essay, "The Myth of the Latin Woman:/Just Met a Girl Named Maria" by Judith Ortiz Cofer. While taking some graduate courses at Oxford

University, Cofer tells how a young man "obviously fresh from a pub," spontaneously knelt down in a bus aisle to face her, put his hands over his heart and bellowed several stanzas. Of Puerto Rican heritage, the author goes on to describe many incidents in her life where others made broad assumptions about her character and even occupation based on her Latina looks.

Perhaps because of my fair complexion, I was spared the worst of what Cofer experienced—the double whammy of ethnic stereotyping based on name and physical appearance. Because all Latinos and Italian Americans have olive skin, don't they?

Soon after the success of Sondheim's "Maria," another, very different Maria song captivated the public, Rogers and Hammerstein's perky "How Do You Solve a Problem Like Maria?" from *The Sound of Music*. But wait a minute—this Maria wasn't Latin like the star-crossed lover in *West Side Story*. She was born in Austria, of all places, and the lyrics told the story of the real-life Maria von Trapp, a would-be nun who became a baroness and leader of the Trapp Family Singers. It was amazing to me to learn that my first name wasn't popular only in the Latin world but also throughout Western and Eastern Europe, Russia, and Greece.

By the mid to late sixties, being Maria was no longer exotic in my Queens neighborhood. Demographics were changing and American society was beginning to move away from its fixation on WASPs. In smart circles, Italians and sometimes even Italian Americans were viewed as creative trendsetters, admired for their talent and rich contributions to the worlds of art, film, cuisine, fashion, and design. I consider myself incredibly fortunate that I had the chance to promote this creativity in the 1970s and early eighties as a young editor at two Italian American magazines, *I-AM* and *Attenzione*.

Despite what appears to be progress in the appreciation of ethnic differences, one fact remains: Italian names still aren't automatically considered desirable. "I'm afraid my daughter has gone over to the Dark Side," my friend Christine admitted with a rueful smile one day. She explained that her daughter, whom I knew as an accomplished, professionally successful 30-year-old engaged to be married, planned to give up her surname. Raised in a proud Italian American home—her father had emigrated from Naples as a boy—she preferred not to keep her name or combine the two last names but to live forever after with the surname of her Irish American husband. Their son, born several years later, was christened Tristan. I was glad to tell Christine that the Tristan Quilt, one of the world's earliest surviving quilts, was sewn in Sicily, home of her paternal grandparents. "So the Italian connection isn't entirely lost," I said.

The Anglo Saxon name of my friend's grandson shouldn't have surprised me. In my family and my Italian American husband's, the grandchildren of our closest relatives are Kate, Jack, Jay, Todd, MacKenzie, Nicole and Brandon.

Any annoyance I may feel about other people's syllable-drop-ping and "de-ethnicizing" is misplaced because I've been guilty of the same tendency. When I became engaged to William Terrone, I saw some kind of cosmic fate in the joining of "round" Rotondi with "earth" (terra/Terrone). But I never hesitated to drop Rotondi for good. Soon after, I eliminated Anna from my birth name on all legal documents. The Maria Terrone that emerged was a svelte, confident, modern woman not even distantly related to the shamed, shrinking person in that fourth grade classroom. When stating my name over the phone and even in person, I was always amused when I was misheard and suddenly became Marie Tyrone, that bonny Irish lass. Such a mistake would never happen to Annamaria Rotondi.

Many years later after both Italian American magazines folded for lack of advertising support and I had paid my dues at two Fortune 500 companies, I began a new communications career as a college administrator. Hired as director of public relations, I was ecstatic to find myself working for the first time in an environment that respected learning and where I would meet interesting, talented and even brilliant scholars and teachers from so many fields. One of the faculty members I got to know was the chairman of the department of Romance Languages, a native of Southern Italy.

After lunch and a few meetings, Pino casually said to me, "You know about the meaning of 'Terrone' to Italians, don't you?"

"I don't understand," I responded, taken aback.

Pino broke the news: the name I'd gladly substituted for my maiden name was a slur, a term used by Northern Italians to belittle Southerners as lazy, crude, ignorant peasants—or even worse. From the neutral "terra"—someone belonging to the land—the name had morphed into a terrible insult.

I was stunned.

For weeks I couldn't stop thinking about this revelation, which felt like a crushing weight, a blow to my slipped-on identity as the confident and modern Maria Terrone. And then I remembered my husband mentioning decades earlier that his Italian-born grandmother used to instruct him and his first cousins, "If anyone insults your name, you can assume that person is from the North. Just answer, "Go *mangiare* your polenta." Why would anyone put down the Terrone name? That question had briefly occurred to me but immediately I dismissed the anecdote as Old World lore, surely nothing that was relevant to me.

Ignorance has its bliss, but that stage was over.

From the "Racial Slur Database" (yes, it exists and covers the world's people):

Terrone—"Any Italian living south of Rome. Very offensive."

From the online "Urban Dictionary":

Terrone—A derogatory term for Italians south of Bologna. Literally translated it means "farmer." Northern Italians use the term with contempt for their uneducated and cultureless brother of the south of Italy.

Examples of use: "Hey, look at that stupid fuckin calabrese. What a terrone. He should go back to his farm and harvest his fuckin eggplants.

How could I have been oblivious of this for so long? It seemed that my desirable two-syllable surname was an insult not just to my own identity but to millions of others, including my Sicilian and Neapolitan ancestors. My head reeled; I was back in the fourth

grade, feeling embarrassed and diminished. When visiting northern Italy with my husband on editorial assignment for *Attenzione*
magazine, I now wondered if the hotel desk clerks had silently
snickered when we checked in. After trying to come to grips with
the Terrone bombshell, I consoled myself with the thought that
99 percent of the people I met in the U.S. wouldn't know about
the negative meaning behind my name. Italian Americans I've
encountered whose names translate as "drunkard, slave and little
dick" probably take similar comfort.

Still, it was the all-encompassing denigration embodied in
Terrone that rankled. At the same time, my interest in my heritage grew, and a few trips to Southern Italy and Sicily affected
me to the core. I found myself attending lectures, watching films
and reading about the Mezzogiorno in an attempt to make up
for the huge gaps in my education. I didn't blame my parents for
that. My American-born mother rebelled against the old country
her entire life. And my father, whose parents emigrated from the
Naples area, was orphaned at a young age and raised by nuns. So
it's not surprising that neither had any special interest in Italy or
things Italian.

And then one day Anthony Tamburri, dean of the Calandra
Italian American Institute in New York, gave me a book whose
very title startled me: *Terroni: All That Has Been Done to Ensure
that the Italians of the South Became "Southerners,"* Italian journalist
Pino Aprile's tenaciously researched and documented book. Aprile
piles up evidence demonstrating that the unification of Italy over
150 years ago was achieved at a severe cost to the South.

Chapter 1, "Becoming a Southerner," was the most shocking.
The author equated what the Piedmontese inflicted on the South
with the crimes of the Nazis, revealing that the first-ever concentration camps in Europe were put into operation by Northern Italians
to torture and kill Southern Italians. He writes that Southerners
were often incarcerated without formal charges or trial and that
prisoners, who "numbered in the hundreds of thousands, were
considered brigands by definition because they were from the
South." Savoy troops massacred huge numbers of citizens, burned

towns, and forced countless peasants to abandon their land—all in the name of unification.

Today's struggling, perpetually under-resourced South was not always that way, I was surprised to learn. In fact, the sprawling, independent Kingdom of the Two Sicilies (1815-1860, a union of the Kingdom of Sicily and the Kingdom of Naples) was an economic powerhouse, "one of the most industrialized countries in the world," Aprile writes. "It stood in third place behind England and France prior to the invasion." But then the Northern invaders emptied not only the wealthy Southern banks, but also palaces, museums and even private homes, he says. Following Italy's unification in 1861, government leaders taxed Southerners at a higher rate and kept resources in the North. In just decades, the neglected South descended into abject poverty.

I could feel my blood rising as I read about this subjugation and complex, unnerving history, which put into context the massive migration of Southerners after unification. An Italian government study estimated that between 1881 to 1927, more than nine million Italians had left the country—one fifth of the total population. Naturally, the overwhelming majority of immigrants were Southerners. After suffering so many losses, the South was being drained of its own people, those with the energy, initiative and courage to remake their lives in a foreign land.

Terroni, a big seller in Italy, opened my eyes to a history that had been suppressed. The book enraged and inflamed me. And because of my married name, it has had a profound personal effect, ultimately empowering me to embrace my Southern Italian roots. A journalist at the Italian daily *Il Corriere della serra* called *Terroni* "a banner book, a flag of the new pride of the South . . ."

Pride—now that's a word to turn the tables. I think of the word "queer," once used as a homophobic slur but neutralized and now used as a positive term in mainstream culture. This reversal came about because gays slyly and ironically appropriated the term for their own purposes.

Southern Italians are doing exactly the same. In a growing pride of their origins, they are using the Terrone slur to proudly and fervidly identify themselves. The Internet, and I suspect, shops all over Southern Italy, are offering many kinds of T-shirts emblazoned with TERRONE in large bold-face type, as well as "Orgoglio Terrone" (Terrone Pride), "100% Terrone," "Calabria Terrone," "Puglia Terrone," "Terrone—Made in South Italy," etc.

But my favorite is this defiant manifesto imprinted not only on T-shirts, but also sweatshirts, hoodies and coffee mugs:

> *"Call me Terrone, muddy my city, insult me if you wish, but I will not bend, I will not keep my head down . . . I am a Terrone and proud of it!"*

I smile when I picture myself wearing this—both personal name tag and a nation's flag—fist clenched, arm raised high.

IV. AT WORK:
FACTORIES AND FIFTH AVENUE

THE CHEMICAL COMPANY

Even if the day was sunny, the air would seem to darken the longer we drove and the farther we bore into the industrial zone. The red brick factories built in the early 20th century were still holding on then, producing staples, electrical circuits, distributor caps and who knows what else. Yet I recall no workers on the streets. There were no stores, no streets, no sidewalks, just ruts. It's as if the factories were run by ghosts and the only evidence of life was an occasional wisp of smoke rising into gray haze.

I was 19, working my last summer job before I married the following June after my junior year of college. Every weekday morning, I'd begin the journey—for it was a journey to a strange land, not a "commute"—with a ride on the elevated train from my home station in Queens. Soon we left behind the residential neighborhoods with their neat houses and orderly street grid. As we approached Long Island City, the factory buildings closed in on us, nearly scraping the slow-moving train. Once through a grimy, broken window I saw a blouse suspended in the hot breath of a standing fan and couldn't tell if the arms strangled or hugged as the blouse twirled in a kind of daze on its huge hook.

I left the train at the appointed stop and waited on a bench on a traffic island, joining a few year-round secretaries also employed by the Philip A. Hunt Chemical Company. Our destination had a street address, I suppose. But the building was located so deep within that desolate wasteland that female workers weren't expected to venture there alone on foot. (Whether the zone was considered too dangerous or the address impossible to find was never explained.) And so the company arranged for a driver to pick us up in a black van, depositing us at the building entrance and retrieving us at 5 pm.

On that small triangle of land, where cars, taxis and buses whizzed by on both sides, I felt safe. Life was normal, civilized: people stopped in delis, glancing at headlines and sipping coffee as they emerged, then striding off with purpose. When Joe, the driver, appeared, he could have been a native guide leading Lewis & Clark into the wilderness. Quickly the bustling streets were swallowed up, the Manhattan skyline just across the East River disappearing as if it had been a mirage. Although we probably took the same route daily, there were no identifying markers along the way—everything seemed to go blank. If I'd been kidnapped and blindfolded, I would have told the police all I knew, that we bumped over cratered streets. We may as well have been on the dark side of the moon.

The Philip A. Hunt Company in New Jersey manufactured chemicals for photo processing and the film industry, but chose to locate an office outpost in Long Island City. The place was like an above-ground, windowless bunker. Having read Sartre's *No Exit* in college, I often thought of that desperate, existential tale as I filed papers and typed letters about chemical orders. Who was I trapped with? And was this for eternity?

I recall only four co-workers: Mr. Sorenson, the suited executive with a vaguely Scandinavian accent, a kind of visitor-emissary from headquarters who was always on the move; Lana, his outpost secretary, who kept her own counsel and, for the entire summer, wore the same navy blue dress and navy blue suit on alternating days, which made me wonder about her salary. And then there was Sheila, the bookkeeper, and Mildred, a typist. Kindly, middle-aged women, they seemed to sense my loneliness and unease, taking me under their wing.

In the airless, unadorned room where we ate our brown-bagged sandwiches—of course, there was nowhere else to eat—they talked about their husbands and grown children, giving me their own recipe-marked cookbooks as farewell presents at the end of that summer. In their gentle solicitousness and desire to pass on their knowledge, they reminded me of Blanche, a supermarket co-worker I met on another summer job.

Sheila and Mildred were the one bright spot in my days, whose minutes were heavy weights dragging across the endless desert of eight hours. Once at lunchtime, I thought I'd try stepping out for a change of air, only to flee back inside to escape the pervasive, stomach-turning odor that reminded me of hot dog food left out to spoil.

When a siren pierced the air for many minutes, its urgency apocalyptic, I overheard Mr. Sorenson talking in a low tone to Lana about a serious accident that had occurred within the zone. Some other office workers—who remain faceless in my memory—began to whisper about fatalities. I had envisioned the other buildings as sealed off, too, their occupants hidden, and so, as if telephones didn't exist, I wondered how the bad news had reached us. Another time, seeing light flash too brightly off a typewriter's metal carriage, I silently panicked, my mind leaping to one thought: nuclear blast. Every dust mote lay suspended and I felt that I was watching myself under a glass dome where I would no doubt die with Lana, Mildred and Sheila, my *No Exit* companions. Less than a minute later, the office soundtrack—speech, typing, shuffling of papers—returned.

That summer job was the toughest—harder than my job as a Dictaphone typist at the V.A. over the previous two summers, where I listened to the psychiatric reports of outpatient veterans. At the V.A. at least I could escape at lunchtime into the "real world" of Manhattan streets. I had no such release at the chemical company, where I lost any sense of control or self-determination. Taken in. Led out. Taken in. Led out.

In the immediate years afterwards, searching for full-time employment during the city's bankruptcy, I compared all job prospects to that experience working in a dying industrial zone that, happily, has vanished.

BLANCHE IN BALANCE

I picture Blanche with white hair to match her French name. I'm quite sure that was true. I also see her wearing a short-sleeved white uniform of nylon or other synthetic fabric, but I must be wrong about that. Would a supermarket cashier be required to impersonate a nurse? Highly unlikely. As a 15-year-old working with Blanche on my first summer job, I didn't even wear an apron embroidered with the "Met Food" logo.

She was kind and maternal and seemed to glow with light. That may seem a ridiculous image, more appropriately applied to haloed saints and Vermeer maidens beneath high windows, making lace or pouring milk from a jug. But to me, perpetually nervous in new situations, she was serene, sweet-natured and seriously professional towards a job that I would have dismissed in my adolescent ignorance as too low-level to merit pride.

I had mixed feelings about having to work at that supermarket on dreary Roosevelt Avenue directly under the screeching elevated train. Besides, its location was inconvenient. In my search for a summer job, I'd stopped in and out of every supermarket within walking distance of home, offering not fleet fingers on the cash register but the warmest smile I could muster. Nada. The next step was to enlarge my hunt on an imaginary map, the way the military or a homicide squad might plot to trap an elusive target. Expanding the search meant riding the subway round trip, buying two tokens every day, knowing that if I were to receive a job offer, I'd have that much less take-home pay from an already meager minimum wage. And so when this particular store needed a cashier and offered to hire me despite my lack of experience, I was relieved but not thrilled. A few of my friends had relatives in high corporate positions who had gotten them cushy jobs in Manhattan offices that summer. Although cashiering at Met Food wasn't a dream job like theirs, I thought it wouldn't be a nightmare, either.

"Show the girl the ropes," the harried manager ordered Blanche on my first day. After demonstrating how the ancient-looking, bulky register functioned, Blanche stood by my side as I rang up a loaf of bread for my first customer. What a shock—I'd charged the man $450, a sum that he loudly protested. Blanche immediately rescued me, using humor to deflect his anger while I thought unkindly, "What kind of moron would actually believe we were charging him that amount?" Then she showed me, with the greatest patience and tact, how to correct my error—exactly what I needed, because underneath my poker face, I was humiliated, asking myself, "How hard can it be to operate a cash register?"

Blanche also made a point of showing me how to pack groceries carefully, dividing the heaviest items over several bags, using a quick mental scale of weights and measures. This lesson, which appears trivial and mundane, reverberated for me then and even now because it indicated a sweeping world view based on consideration for others. "It's so important not to overload anyone," Blanche advised. With a glance, I learned to assess the weight of a 28-ounce can of tomatoes vs. a quart of milk or a large bag of rice against a gallon of bleach.

In fact, Blanche balanced lots of things—not only as a physical scale would do but as a scale of justice, for in her view, everyone deserved equal treatment. That included the young mothers struggling with shopping carts and fidgeting toddlers; the boisterous teens stocking up on Coke and sometimes trying to buy beer; women returning from a long day at work, wearing dress-for-success pumps or the rubber-heeled shoes of nurses and waitresses; the elderly who shopped alone, counting out each nickel and penny that they pushed across the rubber belt towards me.

"No one should be burdened by bags that haven't been packed evenly," she said with conviction, explaining that a bag thoughtlessly packed can strain muscles or even throw a back out of whack for weeks or months, which would mean no work and no pay and a hungry family. I wondered if she was speaking from her own experience or that of a close relative. No, I wouldn't want to be the cause of that sad scenario.

In the meantime, Blanche courteously served the steady stream of customers who entered the store. Although she sometimes talked about her grown children and human relationships in general, I don't recall her making any grand statements of philosophy beyond the essential need for balance—which she clearly believed was the right and fair way of doing things and how, it seems, Blanche lived her life. Like the people who stood on her check-out line, I felt that Blanche eased what could have been a burden for me. What I now think of as her unified world view made all the difference, and I left Met Food in late August not weighed down with resentment for having spent my summer ringing up groceries.

LAND OF THE WOUNDED: A GIRL IN THE V.A.

Entering the Veterans Administration lobby, I was overwhelmed by its sprawling WPA mural that celebrated work and freedom, cities rising bolt to beam, the red-blooded and able-bodied. Everywhere I looked, brawny men hoisted iron, their steel muscles rippling—a Depression-era vision of boundless strength and optimism. And then inside the elevator, I saw the operator, a man with one arm. He sat on a small, low stool and kept up a cheerful banter during his endless exertions—manually pulling open and closed a metal accordion inner door and outer door as he stopped on every floor, workers streaming in and out.

It was the first day of my first full-time, "grown-up" summer job. A classmate and I had scored high enough on the civil service exam offered at our all-girls parochial school to clinch decently paying employment. Working at a Manhattan office struck me as an improvement over my supermarket cashier's job the summer before.

Our V.A. work site was an old building on Seventh Avenue and 25th Street in what straddled then-seedy Chelsea and the still-thriving but gritty Garment District. After the first week, I lost touch with my classmate. She worked somewhere else in that building. If this were science fiction, I'd say that she had gone to live in another zone or quadrant, probably as alien as the one I was assigned to, but altogether different. And it wasn't long before I realized that I needed to summon all my capabilities just to hold body and soul together, so I adopted the self-imposed isolation of a stoic.

My assignment: the Dictaphone Unit responsible for transcribing psychiatrists' reports of veterans' outpatient visits and group therapy sessions. At the supermarket, long before the scanning of bar codes was possible, my fingers ached from pounding the keys down on the heavy cash register. In this job, my fingers would punch typewriter keys for seven hours, but my feet and ears were also engaged. For those who have never heard of Dictaphones—once considered advanced office technology—they were tape players with a wire that led to the ear, and another wire that connected to a foot pedal. Users played the tape, typing the words heard through an ear jack, stopping to advance or rewind the tape with one foot as needed. In this way, hands were always left free to type.

I'd just turned 16 two months earlier and as a striving writer, was hungry for every impression and experience beyond my sheltered life so far. But to be immersed in the intimate problems of veterans for hours at a time—a child who hadn't known real sorrow, men or war—was to inhabit a complex and sometimes disturbing world. I was physically tethered to their stories through the Dictaphone, which I came to regard as a Pandora's Box of secrets.

To be privy to another human being's inner life was hard enough. But these patients were all men and, in my limited experience, males didn't talk about their problems. Now, hearing about rages, alcoholism, the frustrations of chronic pain, impotence and so many other struggles, my mind shrunk away, then reeled. All the while, my right foot pumped the pedal like a piston and my fingers tapped, a super-fast machine.

Whatever knowledge I thought I had about human suffering came through my love of film and literature, the awareness that all good stories need conflict. In the family, when tragedy moved in, the adults held it at a remove, as if shameful. "He has cancer," I once heard my mother tell her sister in hushed tones, referring to a neighbor. The stigma of mental illness went even deeper. When my cousin's wife became psychotic after giving birth to her first and only child, the family closed ranks, a few relatives taking turns to care for the baby. For "outsiders," they invented creative excuses along the lines of "Laura had to be with her dying mother in Oregon," which usually stopped further questions.

I worked in a large room painted bile green with 14 other Dictaphone typists, all full-timers, all sitting at identical gray steel government-issued desks with In Boxes stacked high with tapes each morning. Despite all of these office mates, the ear plugs kept me—and everyone else—cut off from one another. Every desk was like a separate landing field. New tapes came and went, but each typist held her ground, listening to the stories of one veteran after another. It was literally a head-to-toe, whole-body experience. Although I knew the men were supposed to be receiving therapy to ease their suffering, I wondered if they were actually being helped.

I began to feel like a reluctant witness, as if I were nine years old again, back in the children's wing of the hospital, having cracked my skull on pavement. It was not sleeping in an institutional setting for the first time that shook my world, but what I had seen and heard, alone in the night: a distraught toddler repeatedly crying out for someone to retrieve his fallen teddy bear, and the nurse growling threats. Plugged in, listening to each veteran's painful story, I felt the same isolation of the witness.

Over the course of that summer, many vets returned for regular appointments with their therapists. I found myself wondering about, then anticipating with some curiosity how Pete might be coping with his night sweats, Tom with his drinking, and John with his anger and marital conflicts. But by the end of each day, my ears ached and head throbbed with their troubles as they retread the same scorched ground. Occasionally the doctors had the outpatients speak directly into the tape, and their agitated voices were like the sounds of drowning men thrashing in the well of my ears.

The oldest men were World War II veterans, my father's generation, and others had served in Korea. The Vietnam War was in its early stages. Not many of its soldiers had returned yet or, if they had made it back, decided against turning to Uncle Sam for help with their demons. The few Vietnam vets who did visit felt like brothers to me because the standard DOB information on the doctors' reports indicated they weren't much older than me or my brother, Bob—at 19, in college, he was beginning to worry about being drafted.

The vets whose voices I heard helped me imagine their faces. The youngest ones had beards, moustaches, sideburns and long hair, of course—the full-blown hippie styles they were denied in the service. I was sure that the polite World War II guys looked like my dad—clean shaven, wearing glasses, buttoned-down shirts, maybe a little overweight. But unlike my father, who served as a medic in the 16th Armored Division in Europe but never discussed that time, they did talk, at least during their one-hour sessions. I was saddened but initially surprised that decades after the war had ended, they still were struggling with the horrors of the experience. I hadn't heard of post-traumatic stress—I'm not sure PTSD was in the general vocabulary then—but I learned in a visceral way that it's not always possible to "snap out of it and move on."

Facing all 15 of us was Rose, our supervisor. Meeting me for the first time, she mentioned that she had won the Harvest Moon ballroom dance contest several times. I thought it was strange that she bragged about her dancing skills and displayed competition photos and award plaques on her desk. But maybe it was to announce, "Although I'm in this dreary job, probably for the rest of my life, I am far more than this."

Petite and compactly built with a blonde, every-hair-in-place "coiffure," Rose wore bright-colored high heels that clicked loudly as she flounced up and down the rows, surveying our progress—so different from the nuns in elementary and high school who padded along silently before swooping down to announce some infraction. On the days that she wore red or blue dresses, they seemed like billowing flags. The president, Lyndon Baines Johnson, grim-faced on the wall, regarded us all.

Rose was benign, all the while encouraging her "ladies" to increase daily production, measured by the number of tapes moved to the Out Boxes. I remember the embarrassment I felt when she held me up as an example of efficiency—"and she's just a summer employee," Rose said, emphasizing my separateness. Still I was relieved that my co-workers showed no hostility towards me. I chatted with them during the ten-minute morning and afternoon coffee breaks. Never did we talk about the material we were privy to.

That summer of '67, there were over 465,000 members of the armed forces in Vietnam. More than 12,000 Americans had been killed by then and 70,000 wounded. Before the Internet, of course, newspapers were the main source of information, reporting daily the names of the missing, dead and wounded from the metropolitan area and describing, in great detail, the latest land, air and sea battles with the Viet Cong.

Reviewing archived *New York Times* articles returned me immediately to that time. On July 3: *51 Marines Killed in Fierce Battle Near Buffer Zone;170 Wounded.* On the same day: *U.S. Casualties Exceed Saigon's.* July 18: *611th U.S. Plane Downed in North.* July 23: *Budget Deficit Hits $9.9 Billion as War Costs Rise; Second Highest Since WW II.* And another: *President Johnson: "This is Not the Time to Alter Scope of Bombing Pressure."*

The newsstand in the lobby carried all the New York dailies, and the headlines almost always shrieked bad news. Anti-war protests were becoming angrier and more frequent. And another kind of war with its own casualties raged at home that summer: riots spreading from city to city, domestic combat zones that led to the deployment of 1,700 Army troops in Newark and Detroit. Before long, the papers were reporting those dead and wounded, too.

For the two months I worked at the V.A., I didn't have a single exchange with any of my co-workers about the war in Vietnam or at home. For myself, such conversations probably would have pushed me over the edge where I teetered, fighting waves of emotion that ranged from sorrow and frustration to rage at life's unfairness. And so our banter stayed safely apolitical.

A few feet to my left sat Doris, who had once dreamed of being an actress but abandoned auditions long before. I wondered if the stories she heard and transcribed, so full of drama, conflict and complicated relationships, were like plays to her. I felt that way about the veterans I began to "know" that summer. How would their stories end? I wouldn't be there long enough to find out, but maybe the full-timers wouldn't learn the endings, either. Maybe there were no endings, just the ongoing struggle.

On the other side of me was Sheryl, a former gospel singer. "I don't believe in any of that stuff now," she said, and I supposed she meant she no longer went to church. Sheryl seemed to have several boyfriends and loved dancing to soul music on weekends. Sometimes, running into her in the elevator, I heard her humming or singing under her breath. But like everyone else in the unit, she became silent once she was plugged into her Dictaphone. Removing the ear jack for a bathroom break was to hear only the stop-and-start tap of feet on pedals and the bells of typewriter carriages.

I worked in the Land of the Wounded. Some of the outpatients were on crutches or wore bandages and splints. For others, the damage was internal but their eyes gave them away, like one unforgettable supermarket customer I had the summer before, a handsome young man who told me in a conspiratorial whisper, as I rang up his groceries, that he had just returned from "Nam." His blue eyes had a kind of crazed radiance, as if he couldn't quite believe his escape. I thought of him again, wondering if he were now one of the outpatients.

In the cafeteria, the World War II-era cashier was blind, and I wondered about the government's touching faith in the honesty of diners who had to state the denomination of the bills they placed in his hand. I used the cafeteria only on days of heavy rain, preferring to eat a brown bag lunch at my desk to maximize my free time outside. There was no shortage of discounted clothing stores nearby. In my brief break to freedom, I felt almost giddy as I examined racks of paisley miniskirts, orange tunics and striped bell-bottom slacks, treating myself to a purchase after every biweekly paycheck—a complete disconnect from life inside the building. Even during New York's most unbearably hot and humid days, those 50 minutes brought me back to the "normal" world I'd return to at home in the evening and strengthened me for the hours of work that lay ahead.

I spent one more summer at the V.A.—same Rose, same full-timers. The war had escalated by 1968, and I noticed that I was hearing more psychiatric reports on the Vietnam vets, more references to battles with drugs, more prescribing of pills. There was no escaping war or its aftermath, which the vets carried back home. The war was also becoming personal for me. Ricky, a red-haired, freckle-faced kid I grew up with, was in Vietnam then, and so was my cousin Michael (a cigarette lighter in his chest pocket later deflected a well-aimed bullet). The next year, the draft conducted by lottery would hover like a bird of prey over Bob and Bill, the boyfriend who would become my husband.

Recently, trying to learn the fate of that V.A. building, I found a reference in a 1998 *New York Times* real estate article. "An old Veterans Administration ambulatory care center, at the southwest corner of Seventh Avenue and 25th Street, is being converted into housing," I read. Although curious, I can't bring myself to return to that location, knowing it will be unrecognizable, the lobby mural probably whitewashed or much more likely, the entire building torn down by now and replaced with a luxury high-rise.

I felt lucky when I was assigned to the V.A., knowing it meant a steady summer paycheck, but my compensation was long-lasting. My experience with the veterans began as a disembodied physical connection running through a wire to my head and evolved into a much deeper connection, which has continued to pull me towards those profoundly affected by war.

In 1995 on a train ride from Bath to London, my husband and I had a chance encounter with a former Japanese prisoner of war in Burma. For two hours, Fergus Anckorn, a slightly built, soft-spoken man, held us spellbound as he recounted his harrowing experiences. Bill and I hung on every word, oblivious to everything else—the passing scenery, the conductor's announcements and the flow of passengers on and off the train, the heat, our own hunger and thirst. As soon as we returned to our hotel, we wrote furiously, combining what we both recalled to reconstruct, as faithfully as possible, his story.

"I never hated anyone, even when I was being beaten," he said. "Almost all my mates died—it wouldn't be right for them if I spent my life hating, would it?" As he shook his head slowly several times, a strand of sandy-gray hair fell onto his brow, and I noticed then his face was nearly unlined.

Fergus told us that he had recently traveled to Japan with other veterans on the invitation of their government. "We were treated like heroes wherever we went. We talked to schoolchildren, everyone we met, even some former prison guards. Most people had no idea of what had happened to us—they wept when they heard our stories. Some people here, even our vets, criticized me for befriending the Japanese, saying I dishonored the memory of those who died. I feel the opposite. I blame no one. It was just the war."

I hadn't written down contact information or even noted the spelling of his name, but tracked Fergus down after we returned home, and we have been in touch ever since—now by email. Participating in a peace-themed poetry reading, I had the opportunity to tell his story. He's 97 now, but up until his late 80s, he traveled the world, speaking in his quiet, deliberate way to people of all ages and beliefs. I can't help wondering if the American veterans whose stories I heard were also able to put their demons to rest, and why war burns some to hatred and cauterizes others to forgiveness.

Once while browsing in the library, I came upon *After the Noise of Saigon*, the first poetry collection of Walt McDonald. Reading that the author served as a U.S. Air Force pilot from 1957 to 1971 and was then a college professor of poetry, I once again felt an overwhelming need to make contact. This time it was easy. For several years, we exchanged long letters about the writing life.

In his first letter to me sent by U.S. mail and dated September 9, 1998, he wrote: "I came to poetry late, as a middle-aged Air Force pilot, after Vietnam. After some of my friends went off to Vietnam, and one was shot down, then another, I felt a need to say something to them, or about them. I turned to poems when nothing else worked; I could talk with their wives or widows, but my first stumbling attempts were like letters to the dead, or to someone unable to hear, like a poem I wrote for my little daughter when I got my own orders to Vietnam . . . As a young pilot, when I applied to teach English at the Air Force Academy, all I wanted to do was hang around some of the best-used language in the world, some of the most moving, exciting words I'd ever heard—and to share them with others."

Words are what make the difference, I realize, thinking about that summer at the V.A. Isn't that what the so-called talking cure is all about? Isn't that why I have to write about my summers at the Veterans Administration now? The outpatient vets came, the psychologists and psychiatrists summarized the sessions in their oral reports, and I played my role recording them. Words and more words—and I wonder, where are those words now and the lives behind those words?

My mother had told Bob and me as children that my father won her heart by his eloquent letters written almost daily as he rode through Europe with his convoy. As Alzheimer's began to rob him of language, I steeled myself and took the plunge, not knowing what to expect from the veteran who never talked about the war. I untied the fragile blue ribbons around the bundled letters, and read them one by one. A few letters a week become one a day, essential to my father as breathing. "*Though there may be noise and confusion all around, reading a letter from you lifts my heart with an intense joy,*" he wrote. I don't have my mother's replies, but later on my dad wrote: "*Love is a fire that must be nourished or it will die.*"

From Normandy, Poland, Czechoslovakia his truck rumbled, and every day, he wrote his thoughts down, sealed the enveloped and mailed the letter off across the ocean. In ravaged Rouen, where dad carried messages to a hospital, then lost his way back, he wrote:

"*I passed blocks of debris, the spot where St. Joan of Arc died, a French soldier making a watercolor painting of a ruined church—then all at once I found myself where I wanted to be. Now it is late evening, darling. I sit here, reading your letter over and over. Tell me you won't lose courage.*"

I believe that it was the courage of the wounded who kept returning, week after week, seeking solace and some kind of meaning that made such an impression on the girl I was, and the woman I was to become.

THE BEAUTY COMPANY

Leaving the subway at the usual stop near my office, I once found myself stepping into the Jazz Age. Parked all along Central Park South were massive "roadsters" with running boards, and standing under the Plaza Hotel's ornate iron canopy was Christopher Walken in a white zoot suit. Lights, cameras: a film shoot was underway.

That unexpected scene might seem glamorous, but we've all read about the tedium of filmmaking (take 15!), a tedium visible on the actor's face as he awaited the director's cue. I had the feeling that at any moment, Walken might transform into the threatening, unhinged character he plays so well.

Glamour and threat—that scene could be a metaphor for my work as a copywriter at Avon Products, the beauty company a block away, just off fashionable Fifth Avenue.

"The Cast"

1. Brielle

Panther Princess. She who devours men—and women. Breathless baby girl. She whose worker-servant trails her into the elevator, trying to balance a tottering tower of her newly purchased shoes.

She came from somewhere in the Midwest and probably spent her days studying old movies—her voice alternated between Marilyn Monroe's and Audrey Hepburn's Holly Golightly. I sometimes imagined that one day I'd catch her unaware, talking on the phone with the gravelly voice of a truck driver. Like Jay Gatsby, she came East and remade herself according to her idea of a big city sophisticate, marrying a doctor a quarter-century her senior (we glimpsed him once, in a tuxedo on their way to a museum gala), and transforming her Manhattan apartment into an art deco movie set (so we heard, for Brie maintained an air of mystery with the lower castes).

Go lightly she did not. In her tiny, prepubescent voice, she could eviscerate the unsuspecting. When an art director failed to find the midnight blue moiré silk blouse she demanded for a fragrance shoot: "Surely *one* fashion house had such a blouse! And why aren't any of you people capable of understanding my vision?" *Before The Devil Wears Prada*, there was Brielle, a *Vogue* editor wannabe.

When Brielle returned from a safari, she hung on her office wall an oversized, close-up photo of a lion devouring another animal. Stripped down to bone and bloody gristle by the lion's jaws, the unfortunate creature was unrecognizable. In the ever-present gloaming of Brielle's office, that image leapt towards us.

2. Marcy

A woman with a secret life.

On vacation in Paris, browsing an exhibition of photos by Deborah Turbeville, I did a double take: an Avon co-worker, obese and proudly naked, stared back at me. Frozen in black and white, the woman—I'll call her Marcy—stood before a fireplace holding an antique doll. The photo had a strange, brooding quality, as if Marcy existed in the isolation of a dream, making it impossible to detect what she was thinking or feeling as she posed for the famous photographer.

Could this really be the same person who worked on Avon brochures the floor below mine? Who art-directed models wearing the latest cosmetics and designed spreads featuring "gold-toned" earrings, Shari Lewis hand puppets and cologne in kitten-shaped bottles?

We'd never spoken, but I knew of Marcy and sometimes noticed her in the cafeteria: a woman in late middle age who wore a 1920s silver bob with straight bangs, black-framed owl eyeglasses before they were considered cool, and always, a black tent dress accented with a jumble of amber and jade. It can't be her! And then I noticed her name at the bottom of the photo.

After recovering from my shock, I asked myself, why not? Marcy had the aura of an original and self-confidence uninfluenced by passing trends or social expectations. She was an art director, if not an artist herself, and dealt with photographers and their agents. So a connection with the celebrated Turbeville wasn't so unlikely.

But encountering that photo left me feeling uneasy, as if I'd accidentally overheard a confidence. Had Marcy agreed to pose nude because she was sure her photos would be exhibited only where no one she knew was likely to see them? But if she didn't want to be exposed, literally and figuratively, then would she have agreed to strip in the first place?

I never said a word to my co-workers. I knew I'd never approach her—avant-garde people can seem formidable—and whisper, "Your secret is safe with me." I'll never know if Marcy cared one way or the other that I'd seen her revealing photo. But I was glad my instinct about her was right and that I'd caught a glimpse of her life outside the company.

3. Sylvie

She of the big shoulders, of the killer power suits so aggressive, she could mow you down at will. Who strode in tandem with Brie on Fifth Avenue, hoping to be photographed for the Times' *"On the Street" Style page. Who trained her voice to a deep, sultry register and was seen knocking on a male employee's hotel door at 11 pm, reciting "come-on" lines from a 1940s movie through the closed door.*

I was in for it. The good-natured manager who had hired me had jumped ship soon after and just like that, my life was filled with dread and foreboding. When Sylvie's staff heard of her transfer to Sales Communications, they danced on their desks, singing, "Ding, dong, the witch is dead, the wicked witch is dead!" She was heading my way and I was trying to stay calm despite my fears.

Months after reporting to Sylvie, I had a vivid dream:

A Ku Klux Klan rally was underway in the street outside my bedroom. I peeked out, hoping not to be seen. Leading the crazed mob of white-robed murderers was my boss, wearing her favorite blue power suit.

Why such a dream when I didn't know anything about Sylvie's political beliefs?

Maybe what stimulated the nightmare was watching her use humiliation to brutalize my favorite art director on the verge of his retirement for "incompetence and laziness."

Or maybe it was Sylvie's surprising skill with knives. A staff artist—her favorite, no less—had invited all of us to a party at his recently renovated apartment. Sylvie, who enjoyed a drink, or two, three or four, ended up perching herself on a kitchen ledge, flinging one Wusthof knife after another into his freshly painted kitchen wall with great precision.

4. Alyson

Boss of bosses. Refugee from Wilkes-Barre, PA, a queen in her director's corner office, who once ordered the art staff to create "a variety of design options" for her child's Halloween costume.

My first day on the job, a production coordinator named Fritz bragged, "I don't have to worry because I'm Alyson's favorite—I'm protected." A handsome young man with flair, he was godfather to her son, and I learned to steer clear of him.

Some days Alyson demanded drama in our communications to the sales reps. "Create a mystery. Use props to tell a story while introducing them to the new products," she said. "Motivate them to turn pages." Did she want a hand gloved in black leather, an overturned bottle of perfume, a shattered mug stained with crimson lipstick, a pool of blood? *What does Alyson really want?* was the eternal question. We had our theories, but were never sure except for one thing: by constantly revising and even reversing her directions, she created more deadline pressure and kept us off balance. And that's the way she liked it. "No worries. It's only a lipstick company," she'd chuckle, a wicked smile crossing her face as we retreated to kick the doors of bathroom stalls.

Still, I can't complain. Alyson put me in charge of researching and writing a book on what makes a top-selling representative. With the help of four freelancers, we covered America, following 27 representatives with up to $84,000 in annual sales each, an enormous sum at the time. They visited customers in suburban subdivisions, small towns, and inner-city housing and sold in hospitals, factories, schools, company offices and small businesses such as florists and laundromats.

Assigning myself to the Northeast that winter, I tramped through ice-crusted farm fields splattered with mud and manure and spent two hours with nursing home customers who were clearly happy to receive the visit, not to mention their rose-fragranced body lotion. I made the rounds of corporate offices at 5 pm, and saw first-hand that these Avon ladies were smart, strong, creative, caring and in some cases, the main support of their families. Several were the only support during their husbands' extended job layoffs.

What I most admired was how much they went out of their way for their customers. One Midwestern representative borrowed her husband's truck to make a delivery in an ice storm, stopping first to pick up milk for the customer. Some women mentioned that their reps had driven them to doctors' appointments. And when one customer suddenly had to leave because of a family emergency, one rep changed her schedule to babysit. On one of the most revealing visits, a representative in Gary, Indiana, recognizing her customer's budget struggles at that time, actually discouraged her from placing a large order. Because of the close relationships of trust that developed, it wasn't unusual for these top-sellers to receive customers' invitations to family weddings and graduations. From my observations and the freelancers', I saw that the reality of the representatives' lives had no relationship to the world of 9 West 57th Street, the distant headquarters they perceived as fairy-tale glamorous.

Ultimately, Alyson changed her mind about publishing the book that I'd titled *Selling With Heart*, despite the huge expenditure of time and money. AIDS, ravaging the city then, killed a talented young art director as well as Fritz, Alyson abandoning him soon after the diagnosis. And poor executive decisions at the company ended employment for hundreds of managers, myself included (ironically, by the time of the layoffs, I'd moved up from lowly copywriter to public relations manager in another division 20 floors up, a heavenly deliverance while it lasted).

Recently I've learned from online searching that Marcy, who must be close to 80 now, sells her own designs—eco-totes, t-shirts, even skirts and dresses in mod colors. She lives in Nebraska. I like to picture a wind-swept prairie and Marcy, still wearing a black tent dress and exotic bangles, opening the door to her local Avon representative with an enigmatic smile. I like to think she still lives a fascinating double life.

V. FROM NEW YORK TO THE WORLD

THE LAST CAR

I was alone on the elevated train when the gang of teenage boys burst in.

It was a late Monday morning in winter, and the train was crawling through the Bronx, where I lived then during the "New York City is bankrupt Bronx is burning" era. The South Bronx was decimated, and a daily tabloid had just published a series on its violent street gangs. The editor characterized one with the headline "THEY KILLED FOR A QUARTER."

The city's economic crash had affected me body and soul. I was a newlywed and naively expected happiness to radiate into every corner of my life. But every morning I'd awaken as if pinned under a heavy weight, conscious of my continuing unemployment after six months of searching, unsure of myself and my future as a recently graduated English major. Those days, even entry-level typing jobs in publishing were scarce, and I was beginning to despair. When I entered the empty last car that day, heading towards Manhattan for a job interview, I was wearing black patent leather shoes, a tweed coat and a brimmed felt hat—prim, proper and wildly conspicuous.

"Never show fear," my brother used to say, advice I thought absurd as a girl because of its irrelevance to my life. Now I heard him urgently whispering those words in my ear as the teens rushed en masse to the opposite end of the car. They were spray-painting every inch of wall, working with purposeful efficiency and what seemed like quiet glee, moving closer to me foot by foot.

I began to argue intensely with myself. "They're just kids. Maybe I'm not in danger after all," I suggested hopefully in my most reasoned tones, struggling to stay calm. "Then again, graffiti writers are vandals, subject to arrest, and I'm a witness, which makes me a threat, which might put me in the category 'To Be Eliminated.'" I wondered if I should move, but then it occurred to me that getting up and lurching through the moving train into the next car might draw attention to myself, a risk. "It's a chance I have to take! Make a dash for it, or just get up and walk calmly, but do it NOW."

And so my internal debate went, what I think of as my "to be or not to be" musings. I wasn't ready to shuffle off the mortal coil just yet, but I simply couldn't act. And so I remained rooted to my seat, pretending to be interested only in my book. Later I recognized the irony in what I was reading: *Do It! Scenarios of the Revolution* by political provocateur Jerry Rubin. Of course I'd stopped registering meaning the moment the teens entered, for I had suddenly become an unwilling character in an unexpected story, maybe a horror story involving knives and a young victim's blood gushing over her Sunday-best coat. I raised the paperback closer to my face, hoping to disappear.

Every few minutes, the train stopped and its doors opened, giving me hope that someone would enter. But my attempts to influence behavior with telepathy failed. Anyone who stood on the platform quickly sized up the situation and, wanting no part of it, stepped into the adjoining car instead.

The smell of spray paint was getting stronger. I peeked furtively over the top of *Do It!* and saw the aerosol-armed teens were within a few yards. Then one of the boys, who looked all of 15, approached me. "This is it," I thought, my heart pounding as if being played by a deranged drummer, "my last moment on earth." I wished I'd never been asked to interview for the editorial assistant job that day, I wished I was back in bed, safe. But when the boy pointed with his paint can to the wall behind my seat, I knew with a flood of relief that he meant me no harm. Hunching, I bent my head low so that he could spray his tag without interference.

At the next station, job done, they all piled out. My siege of terror was over. During what had felt like an hour but was probably ten minutes, no one had uttered a word to me. After my breathing returned to normal and the car gradually filled with other passengers, I felt a bit sheepish for having thought my life was at stake, but not sheepish to the point of self-flagellation—after all, not one person had the nerve to enter the last car, stop after stop. I was also sure that the experience would stay with me for a long time. Already I could hear myself dramatically recounting to rapt friends the story of my "close call." This surprised me. Only moments earlier, I seriously wondered if my life was about to meet a violent end.

Ultimately, what only mattered to those teenagers was using graffiti to claim the car for themselves. During those grim days, graffiti was a visual symbol of social anarchy and urban blight. To spend time in an enclosed space like a subway car covered with spray paint and black marker was to experience the deeply unsettling feeling of being trapped in Hades. That atmosphere did little to lift me from the gloom and fright of my joblessness and my eroding confidence in myself and a rational world.

Today, some graffiti is readily called art and is even produced for public parks or on the sides of new condo buildings, commissioned by landlords who recognize its appeal to certain markets. But back then, authorities were waging a war on graffiti that young men—for the graffiti subculture was almost exclusively male—found ways to circumvent, even venturing into dangerous tunnels. In graffiti vernacular, the mission was always to "write their tags"—never their own names, but an alias chosen for personal meaning as a way to assert a new identity. Often during my interminable job hunt as I filled out applications, I sighed silently as I signed my name. I too wanted a new self—the successful self I felt I was meant to be because the self I knew wasn't getting anywhere.

It's taken years for me to answer "writer" when someone asks me what I do, despite the many times that I added my name to a poem or essay. These teenagers called themselves writers from the start, asserting their right to be through the "pen names" they took on—but writ large from a spray can or Magic Marker instead of a pen. Like the rest of us, they were probably trying to beat the odds of insignificance, of going unnoticed and being forgotten, of nothingness itself.

From the tunnel of my memory, I'm pulled back to the dungeons of the Doge's Palace in Venice, across the appropriately named Bridge of Sighs, and the names that the condemned had scratched or written on the walls—a final act against the looming void. It strikes me that despite their crimes, real or fabricated by enemies (a frequent occurrence in 16th-century Venice), the graffiti writers Marco, Giuseppe and Antonio have achieved a poignant recognition. Even now, still legible after more than four centuries, their names have the power to unsettle and move the viewer. I stared at them for minutes, imagining the desperate need of those men to declare their very existence.

Thinking about my slow progression through the low-ceilinged, dank and twisting corridor of that prison and the inhuman conditions the inmates endured, I return to the New York City subway and the depressed era of that ride. Besides the stories of vicious street gangs, I also recall many newspaper and TV exposés about crumbling South Bronx tenements and vermin-filled apartments without heat or hot water along that same elevated train route. I knew these horrors existed less than three miles from where my husband and I lived. Our dark apartment near the noisy el train faced a wall, but was located in what was considered a safe neighborhood. Despite my near-desperation over being jobless for so long, I knew I would never descend into poverty, and that whenever I traveled on that train through the devastation, I was just passing by.

My interview that day didn't lead to employment. Eventually, I had a lucky break and landed an editorial job, low paying but providing the career experience I needed for the next job up the ladder. The words "dead end," which had begun to turn up in my mind like hangmen in waiting, suddenly vanished.

Recently I've been wondering about those boys in the last car. Were any of them highly talented, aspiring artists who planned their designs before sneaking into subway yards at night to sign across the car exteriors? No, I'm not glamorizing what they did, but sometimes the multicolored, baroque swirls of names across the entire length of a train had a startling beauty that stopped me in my rush to board. Being only 21 years old myself, I felt and understood the vitality, the youthful declaration of the "I," the "yes!" defying all the "no's" that the writers probably faced elsewhere in their lives. Painted over at first, by now all of that graffiti, the ugly and the beautiful alike, has been crushed and scrapped.

In his book *Graffiti Lives: Beyond the Tag in New York's Urban Underground* (NYU Press, 2011), sociologist Gregory J. Synder writes that some of the graffiti writers "went legit . . . attending college, starting magazines, Web sites and real estate businesses" and pursuing "careers in art and marketing. These kids refused the meager options presented to them by the larger society, and instead perfected extremely risky cultural pursuits," says Snyder. "Their success in this form eventually opened up other opportunities, and today those efforts are paying off, literally."

I can't help wondering about the men those boys have since become, and how else they've left their mark. Did they try out other identities and, like me, run into some luck on the ride?

BEGGARS

Lately I've been thinking about panhandlers, a fact of life in New York. Last week a girl in her twenties was slowly making her way through the subway car, listing the disasters that had befallen her which, she said, had left her homeless. The stories we hear are usually about a serious illness, death in the family, loss of job and shelter, a hungry child to feed. The girl began to pace from one end of the car to the other, imploring "Help me, HELP, HELP until the words became a choking wail that filled the air. Most of us kept our eyes closed or fixed on our phones. I know that, because we, the entreated, are in this together, and that's why I steal furtive glances, wondering how others are, or aren't reacting. What should I think? Or do?

Describing my moral dilemma to a cousin, she recounted one of her own subway stories: an impeccably dressed man holding a clipboard described the tragedy of six-year-old girl in his neighborhood who had been killed—and her grieving parents didn't have enough money to bury her. "Could you find it in your hearts to help them out?" he asked. The tale elicited great sympathy and cash from the riders, many who appeared to be struggling themselves. "Oh no, a month later and she was killed again?" another passenger exclaimed in a tone of withering sarcasm, rolling his eyes. The exposure of this deception, followed by gasps and some laughter, caused the red-faced con man to rush out at the next stop.

That incident occurred years ago before the Transit Authority had produced its piped-in recording reminding passengers that soliciting money in the subway is illegal. "We ask you not to give," says the disembodied voice. "Please help us maintain an orderly subway." Another requests, "Please give instead to reputable charities."

And yet, my faith tells me that the needy are the face of God, and we must give food to the hungry, drink to the thirsty, clothes to the naked. That gets complicated in any big city when during the course of a day, a traveler may pass or personally encounter scores of beggars, some truly needy and others outright frauds. Even the deceivers are quick to say "God bless you" when accepting donations from sympathizers. It can be impossible to tell the difference between them.

*

I can still see the faces of some of the subway beggars I gave to, even years later—the man in tatters with one eye shut and the other bulging eye a startling milky-white and the man in a wheelchair with an ugly festering wound on his calf. With their physical deficits on display, I knew they weren't faking. Once I was overwhelmed by a beggar's dignified bearing that belied the humiliation of his silent supplication:

IN THE LAND OF EMPERORS

He's alive, but halved, on a plank—
head, torso and muscled arms
wheeling down the train platform
to the top of the stairs,
and I stop in my tracks
midway through some rumination
that's instantly replaced by one
about humans made in God's own image.
I imagine the workbench abandoned
in the middle of the job,
some more cursed than others,
forced to eat dust,
denied the chance to run.
I reverse my steps,
read a billboard, wait till it's safe: he's gone.

Still, my legs quiver
on the same steep flight of steel steps
he bumped or slid or rode down
a moment ago, transporting himself
to the next plane, the broken world—
transforming himself.
In marble halls, I've admired
the busts of emperors, larger than life
with their smashed noses and missing limbs.
I know a black king
glides by now on ball bearings,
past sidewalk crowds that part in two.

*

When was their last meal? Isn't it the duty of the privileged to feed those who hunger? I once passed a middle-aged woman beggar sitting on the sidewalk in an affluent Manhattan neighborhood. I was on my way to work, carrying my usual brown bag lunch. Passing her by, I remembered the turkey sandwich on multigrain bread I'd made that morning, and retraced my steps. But when I handed her the foil-wrapped sandwich, she refused it, waving me away, a gesture that fed my cynicism, which seems always to lurk beneath the surface. Naturally, the sandwich was useless. It couldn't buy a bottle of gin or drugs.

Nothing left me feeling more uneasy than the two deaf Latino beggars who entered my subway car in Queens, an incident I remember clearly after two decades. They placed a cheap trinket on the lap of every seated passenger, along with a card announcing their disability and a request to buy their merchandise. As soon as that task was done, they returned to each rider, retrieving the cards and trinkets from those who didn't give. I remember how quickly they moved and how solemn they were, and the sadness mixed with disquiet that I felt watching them.

Later that year, a *New York Times* headline caught my eye: "Seven Arrested in Abuse of Deaf Immigrants." It turns out that those beggars—among a group of 57 including 12 children—had been victims of smugglers who brought them out of Mexico into

New York with the false promise of an honest livelihood "working for a small business." Instead they were housed in a squalid apartment in Queens and forced to sell trinkets in the subway or face beatings, children included. At the end of the day, the money they brought in was turned over to the enforcers. Eventually, a few of the victims worked up the courage at 4 am to leave a letter about their plight at the local police station. I was upset to learn that this happened in my precinct and that these near-slaves had been hidden nearby.

If I'd felt uneasy witnessing those beggars in action—something beyond the fact of their begging seemed "off" to me—I was equally shaken by the victims' proximity to my home. Were there others hidden away from view, suffering terribly, in this place where I grew up, a community I thought I knew?

"The biggest factor that kept them there was their disability, which kept them dependent on the smugglers, and isolated them terribly," said an officer from Immigration and Naturalization Service. "That was their key vulnerability, and the smugglers exploited it tremendously." If I had bought a trinket that day, my money would have gone to the smugglers. But when the deaf beggars brought back too little, they were violently abused. Giving or not giving led to a negative outcome either way.

Like most New Yorkers, I've learned to trust my instincts and make a split-second decision as to whom I should give, knowing that I've probably made plenty of misjudgments over the years.

There are times when I give only because I feel pressured, which leaves me angry with myself and the person creating what I interpret as an implicit threat. Recently, sitting alone toward the end of an empty subway platform, I was approached by a teenage boy with a mask-like, forlorn expression. He came so close that when he extended his open palm, his skin almost touched my face. Aware at that moment of my isolation, I reached into my handbag, careful not to bring my wallet into view, handing him a dollar. Without a word, he swaggered away. His sudden change of gait confirmed my suspicion: I'd been had. Before I could dwell on what had just occurred, a wiry, street-wise-looking guy with earbuds and a backpack appeared on the adjoining bench.

"Did he bother you?" he asked me. "I don't like that shit. I was watching from down the platform and was ready to move in if I had to." I thanked him for his concern, silently grateful for the presence of invisible guardians in our midst.

*

For the first time in a lifetime of exposure to city beggars, I've just encountered a subway poet, "Brian from the Bronx." Dressed neatly in black jeans and a pressed white T-shirt, Brian recited from memory a long, rhyming, lyrical poem about his life and his yearning to become someone who mattered. I only wish I could have recorded the work of this talented writer who was so modest, he didn't even extend his hand as he walked through the car. We could have been at the events corner of Barnes & Noble.

And then there are the musicians. "I don't beg. I entertain New York," the stout old man announced yesterday, smiling broadly and then launching into a one-man version of the Drifters' "Under the Boardwalk," followed by other sixties soul hits. I have a soft spot for all musicians—the Irish folk singer and her companion fiddler, the Andes natives in multi-colored serapes playing pan flutes, the gray-haired doo-woppers moving their hands and feet in choreographed harmony, an electric guitarist at the Herald Square station backed by a wildly expressive violinist, the blues singer as moving as B.B. King, the man tapping a Chinese xylophone gently, as if freeing its spirit, the teenager wearing a gown ideal for a Metropolitan Opera debut singing an aria from *La Traviata*—all the world's music amplified and resonating in the subway's passageways.

Of course, buskers don't consider themselves beggars. I wonder if my Italian-born ancestors living in Manhattan in the early 1900s ever gave a coin to an organ grinder with or without a trained monkey wearing perfectly stitched, handmade clothes? Many of those performers were poor immigrants from Southern Italy who eked out a living for their families, playing and replaying the same few stored tunes. But that ended in 1935 when Mayor LaGuardia banned them, considering the organ grinders to be beggars who added clutter to New York's teeming streets.

*

In the era of boom boxes, the subways were filled with b-boys blasting their favorite funk tunes while they breakdanced with abandon down the aisle. Although I was impressed with the energy and gymnastic skill on display, I have to admit at the risk of sounding like a grouch that I resented their attitude of domination. "It's show time! We're here and we're great!" It may not ever be completely peaceful underground, hurtling with all kinds of strangers in a no-exit situation, but we are usually left alone with our private thoughts, our music, our reading, our endless digital distractions. Not true with the breakdancers whose act takes over our space. We're suddenly with them on the narrow stage of the subway car, like it or not. I think some passengers quickly pay up just to be rid of them.

My attitude hadn't changed when the newest version of subway performer recently appeared in my car: a teenager with one of those trendy blonde Afros who first turned on the music (to my surprise, a long-ago disco hit—loud, but not ear-splitting) and then catapulted his lithe body onto the looped metal rods attached to the ceiling. His acrobatic maneuvers were astonishing. He, too, took over the car, and his quick moves overhead in the tight space made me duck a few times. And yet, in spite of myself, I couldn't help admiring his exuberance and ability to defy gravity like a ballet dancer or Olympic gymnast. And then, head dangling upside down, he reached out and lightly touched the finger of a seated woman. She allowed a faint smile to cross her face.

In the land of beggars, even those who have no legs still manage to overcome the limitations of their bodies. And at least one, I've witnessed, can fly.

Excellent ✓

A PILGRIMAGE TO 5 POINTZ

From the el in Queens, I'd glimpse the phantasmagoria that was 5 Pointz. A riot of color and occasional faces covering every inch of the old, block-long factory, it felt hallucinatory. In a minute—not enough time for the eye or brain to take it all in—the images vanished and the train rumbled underground, heading to Manhattan.

For years, male and female aerosol artists from all over the world—Europe, Australia, Japan— created their graffiti art here, on the outside walls of this meandering, low-rise complex in now-gentrifying Long Island City. (I later learned that curator and graffiti veteran Jonathan Cohen, known as "Meres One," reviewed all artists' requests in advance.) I was intrigued, but although I lived just a short train ride away, I never paid a visit. That is, until 5 Pointz came under threat by its owner-developers, who announced plans to bulldoze and erect two luxury high-rise apartment buildings on the site.

I enlisted my cousin Jerry Rotondi, an avid 5 Pointz fan, to be my guide. Nothing prepared me for the experience. I was stunned by the intricacy of the vibrant images climbing stories high, and their careful planning and execution. What I saw that day was as far from crude "spray and run" graffiti as you can imagine. When I came upon the face of a helmeted soldier painted in pointillism style, I realized I was in an outdoor museum—not the kind where patrons tiptoe, speaking in whispers, but a dynamic, ever-changing creative hub. Even the colors seemed to vibrate.

Besides the energy, there was a palpable sense of camaraderie at 5 Pointz, as artists worked from street level or on ladders while wide-eyed tourists—many foreign-born—snapped away or shot video. In the distance, the crimson logo of the Citicorp skyscraper pierced the clouds in visual counterpoint.

With the threat of demolition looming, "Save 5 Pointz" rallies were held, testimony presented to elected officials, and a lawsuit filed on behalf of the artists. Then in the early hours of November 19, 2013, the unthinkable happened: the landlord had the art whitewashed into oblivion. Word spread and "R.I.P.— REST IN POWER" signs soon appeared.

"I feel the loss emotionally," says Jerry, 72, a retired art director who calls himself a 5 Pointz volunteer, advocate, and friend. "What happened there was real democracy. Artists of all ages, ethnicities and social strata had one thing in common: the creation of an art building unique in the world. It was a pilgrimage site, a meeting place to revel in art, a crucible of creativity."

Jerry tells me that once he overheard a little girl wonder aloud, "Is this Candyland?" I know how she felt. There was something about the place that sparked a feeling of giddy fun, and I found myself constantly gasping in delight, taking photos with abandon. Everywhere I looked, there was an image I wanted to savor.

The initial shock over the loss has passed, but many are still mourning. Years from now, 5 Pointz will be remembered internationally as an artists' mecca like no other. In the meantime, 21 graffiti artists whose work was destroyed and who sued the developer can enjoy the many satisfactions of victory: in February 2018, the judge awarded them $6.7 million.

A FACEBOOK PAGE IN IRAN

I was about to go through security at Kennedy Airport, and my heart was pounding. Had my literary friendship landed me on a U.S. terrorist list?

But all went smoothly. Not long before, the situation was reversed, and I was the one afraid that I'd become a terrorist target. It all began one Saturday night when my husband decided to Google me. On top of the search result was my photo—the same photo on the back of my first poetry collection—surrounded by Arabic writing. What was this? How long had I been under surveillance? And why me, an innocent in Queens, New York?

A click led to a site called *Manhia*, dense with text that could have been poetry—hard to know for sure because of the unrecognizable language and unfamiliar faces. When I came upon T.S. Eliot, it felt like an encounter with a long-lost friend on the street of a foreign city. My palpitations slowed.

I examined the writing next to my photo. Clearly the short lines were stanzas. Was I the author of whatever I was looking at, or could this be a list of reasons in verse of why I had to die?

The "Contact Us" link opened up a blank email to the editor. I dashed one off, asking how I had come to be in this curious place. Within hours, an Iranian ex-pat poet named Maryam Hoole responded from Sweden, explaining that she now edited this literary site in the Farsi language. Mohsen Fathezade, a college student, had translated one of my poems and sent it to her.

I knew no one in Iran and jumped at her offer to forward my email. Lightning-quick, Mohsen responded. He had stumbled on one of my poems on the web—a 9/11 poem, no less. This was all happening just two years after the attack and learning the subject of the translation wasn't exactly calming. Still, I was flattered that my poem about an imagined waiter in nearly deserted Chinatown had an impact on this stranger on the other side of the world. The fact that he was a resident of what George W. Bush had once called "The Axis of Evil" made the connection feel even more amazing.

And connect we did via frequent emails and snail-mailed letters. A native of Shiraz, Mohsen was about to graduate with a degree in engineering, a practical career choice, although his heart had always been with literature. His written English—imperfect but easy enough to understand—was self-taught, and he and I often talked about our favorite authors. Although I was decades older than Mohsen, I felt that we communicated like peers.

How could I not send my "translator"—I loved the very sound of the word—my own book of poetry? I was touched when Mohsen told me that he hoped to publish the poems in Farsi and began asking questions about the meaning of specific lines so that he could "get it right."

Except for those writers asked to commemorate presidential inaugurations, poets are, let's face it, invisible in America. In Iran, I learned, they're revered and some are considered so influential, their writing can land them in jail. So it was a strangely surreal and very heady feeling for me to be interviewed by Mohsen and become the subject of an eight-page feature in *Hengam*, an independent literary supplement. The fact that I couldn't read the Q&A or any of my own poems didn't take away from the thrill.

When the exhilaration of being Iran's literary bold-face-name-of-the-week subsided, I began to stress over the possible conse-quences. I thought about the foreign hikers who had accidentally crossed an unmarked border into Iran and been imprisoned—an innocent act compared to this flagrant promotion of my writing. Had my local post office alerted the Feds after observing the Iranian postmark on the bulky *Hengam* package with its stamps of grim-faced Ayatollahs, lined up in rows like troops? Were the emails between me and Mohsen being monitored in Iran? Were they being monitored in America? My smooth departure at Kennedy told me otherwise.

Mohsen and I continued to correspond over the ensuing years—through his required stint in the army, which he had dreaded; his marriage to his cousin Leila (wedding a cousin, I learned, is a strong tradition); his work building dams for an engineering company. He became a second brother to me. Did we talk politics? Sometimes. He was born after the 1979 revolution that toppled the Shah and installed the oppressive theocracy still in power. Mohsen had experienced nothing else, but thanks to the Internet, he knew what he was missing.

Because of my deepening relationship with Mohsen, I found myself wanting to learn all I could about the history and heritage of his country. Keats had Italy, Shelley had Greece, and I was experiencing a romance with Persia. From our first exchanges, Mohsen spoke very proudly of his ancient heritage and its huge contributions to civilization in the arts, sciences, architecture, and, supreme irony, in human rights. (The Cyrus Cylinder, named after the Persian ruler Cyrus the Great, predates the Magna Carta by a millennium.)

When a gift from Mohsen unexpectedly arrived in the mail—a lavishly illustrated, hard-cover edition of the *Rubaiyat* by the 11th-century poet Omar Khayyam—I plunged into that exotic world. I also read Azadeh Moaveni's hip *Lipstick Jhihad* memoir and the wonderful *Strange Times, My Dear: The Pen Anthology of Contemporary Iranian Literature*. "No amount of pontificating on the ebb and flow of political events in Iran in the last two decades could even begin to account for the fevered mental activity of Iranian poets as they interpret their experiences and emotions . . ." wrote poetry editor Ahmad Karimi Hakkak in his introduction. I also attended lectures and sought out Iranian films both obscure and famous, such as the Oscar-winning *A Separation*.

In 2009, as concerns grew about Iran's possible development of nuclear weapons, I devoured every article and op-ed that I could find. The daily street protests began that year after the questionable reelection of their president—the biggest demonstrations since the revolution. I worried about Mohsen's safety and was deeply affected by the images of wounded and dying protestors that had been tweeted and You-Tubed around the world. We both hoped that dramatic political change would result, but the authorities cracked down hard.

On a personal level, social media is changing Mohsen's life through his embrace of Facebook, where our conversation now takes place (safer from prying eyes than email, he says). He has lost his job with the engineering company—the tougher Western sanctions are working, inflation is in the double-digits and his employers no longer receive the government subsidies that paid his salary. With time on his hands, Mohsen now lives online. Mostly everything on his constantly updated pages is in Farsi. No matter—I can still view the newest photos and the occasional English posting outside of our exchanges, such as his pained lament the day Whitney Houston died.

Becoming immersed in Mohsen's virtual life inspired me to write a poem titled "A Facebook Page in Iran," that was subsequently published in *Atlanta Review*'s annual international issue. Excerpt: *It's raining Farsi here, so hard/I can't see my way//through a fog of curlicues./I bump into Mohsen, trapped//there and he knows it. He knows/the official no-no's, too many to list,//but his page is Fort Defiance,/I'm guessing, each post a tinderbox//of revolution and rock 'n roll, mixed in//with pix of friends looking weird but smart,//rueful smiles from cafes* . . . Without notice, I posted the entire poem on his Facebook page and waited to see what would happen.

Almost immediately, the conversational deluge began. "Oh my Ggggod. It was really surprising when I started to read, then I saw it's about me," Mohsen wrote. And a few hours later: "I was awake all night typing . . . I have too many words for this."

Then Mohsen's friends in Iran, Dubai and Canada chimed in. Several sent congratulations. 286 "likes" were recorded. Via Facebook "friending," I introduced Mohsen to my colleague Roger Sedarat, an Iranian American poet and translator, who had assured me earlier that Mohsen was a graceful translator of my work. I was pleased when the conversation took off about Roger's two Iran-inspired collections and couldn't help feeling that my caprice had led to an international literary salon in cyberspace.

Recently we moved to another stage and began to Skype. The picture is shaky and sometimes breaks down, which seems like a metaphor for his country, but Mohsen's voice is clear and surprisingly lively. "The Iranian people love America," he said earnestly the first time we Skyped. It's hard to ignore the wistfulness in his voice—or is it bravely concealed desperation when he says, "America is my dream"?

Will we ever meet outside the Internet or a video monitor? In our last conversation, Mohsen told me that he's already inscribed an illustrated book of poetry by Hafez for me. "Hold it for the day we'll meet face to face," I suggested. With the election of the moderate cleric Hassan Rouhani as president, Mohsen is optimistic. But with Donald Trump in the White House as of 2017, and his ban on travel from six majority-Muslim nations including Iran, I'm afraid that we may never meet.

"If change is going to come, it must begin with the people," Mohsen says, and he's right. In the meantime, I'm sure of one thing: these two friends will go on talking.

literal

AT HOME IN THE NEW WORLD

I am in a cave below the river. I am in the deepest layer of my buried city, my very own Pompeii. From my earliest memories, I rode the subway, that Vesuvian-roaring underworld built by the Sicilian-born grandfather whom I knew only from photographs—sandhogs they're still called, the men who shoveled and blasted inch by uncharted inch in their passage through the bedrock of a new land. Some survived a long ocean journey only to die here, where the tunnel walls now hold the river back. Looking around, I see some bodies slumped in sleep, faces slackened like blank masks. Others tap their feet to music I can't hear. I am one of many travelers, all of us arriving from somewhere else but hurtling in the same direction.

The doors open: Roosevelt Avenue and 74th Street, Jackson Heights, the neighborhood where I skipped rope, lined up in the St. Joan of Arc schoolyard, pledged my marriage vows—once a calm, predictable, beginning-middle-end kind of place but today a kaleidoscope turning in the hands of thousands, its colors and patterns constantly shifting. A place where "peace and quiet" is elusive and ever more precious when it's found.

I climb steps and more steps to penetrate the layers, moving up, up, and finally into the light. I am in New Mumbai, where light spins off intricate earrings, mirrors scatter across gauzy tunics and tiny silver bells tinkle in an unseen breeze. In that small disturbance of air, the scent of sandalwood wafts like incense. I've been resurrected from my buried city and stand in the open, but I'm dazed, knowing all that I don't know. Once at a Metropolitan Museum photo exhibit on religious practice in New York City, I was transfixed by the black-and-white images of shrines in the back rooms of shops on this very block. Blinded by dazzle, I long to be invited into the shadows.

I try to imagine draping my flesh with rippling, turquoise silk, gold-flecked above a peek of bare midriff, my eyes kohl-rimmed, hair hennaed, feet sandaled even in winter because I carry the subcontinent within me, I shimmer its heat as I stroll down the block to the sounds of Punjabi pop from sidewalk speakers.

Oh, to know each of the 34 jewelers by name, not just the Sikh on the corner whose display board dangles "costume" earrings fit for Bollywood's version of a Cecil B. epic. I'd stride into the 22K-real-thing emporiums, bartering pleasantly, skillfully in one of 2,000 Indian dialects or Urdu or English, that great unifier of the Raj, departing triumphant in my gold filigreed bracelet five inches wide that delicately chains my wrist to a matching ring while popping the eye of every beholder.

And I wonder if I'll ever know the names of the gods and goddesses greeting passersby from their places of honor in those come-hither windows, the flute players and monkey god, the three-headed dogs made of brass and bronze, the four-handed, smiling, pink elephant god.

Food is consolation for more than ignorance, so I plunge into Patel Brothers supermarket, site of the long-gone Key Food during the time when my native Queens was Wonder Bread country. But as a dazed foodie in culinary Xanadu, I face only more questions. I wander aisles packed with tamarind, mango crates, ten-pound sacks of basmati rice, pistachios and cardamom, Ceylon tea and outsize, other-worldly vegetables. Where is my guide?

*

When I pass my neighbors on the sidewalk in our seemingly choreographed chaos, I wonder about their pasts. Sometimes my eyes unexpectedly lock for an instant with the eyes of a passing veiled woman in blue jeans, or my ear will catch a lilting brogue or patois. Six out of ten people I pass on the street in Jackson Heights were born in another land—Ecuador, Peru, Mexico, Bangladesh, Thailand, Ukraine. Did they flee famine? Killing fields? Violent relationships? Or a sudden, political fall from lives of privilege?

Do they line up weekly behind thick glass windows to wire money home for children, parents, wives or husbands left behind? And then I recall my cousin's story of my grandmother shipping pillowcases packed with canned food to her tiny hill town outside Palermo during World War II. This is what immigrants are born to do: face both forward and back, like Janus, one of our many Roman gods.

Am I naïve in thinking that food is the link that can bring us together? Once a member of a group called Chefs for Peace was quoted saying, "*In most kitchens all over Jerusalem or Tel Aviv, there are Palestinians and Israelis cooking together, shoulder to shoulder, with long knives.*" Those knives, crossed daily against ancient stone, keep to themselves. I think that in my neighborhood, right now Pakistanis are chopping onion for chicken biryani in Indian restaurants and vice-versa, working side by side despite decades of enmity and religious conflict.

I yearn to experience the essence of my neighbors through the authentic dishes available for tasting right at my doorstep. This wish probably comes directly from my Italian American heritage with its near-worship of food—not just for its gorgeous sensory appeal, but also as a means to nurture and unite people as members of a local and extended human family. In short, food equals home. Cooking dishes from all over the world, I feel connected to everyone else who ever stood or stands by a kitchen stove or over a fire, stirring a pot.

And so, in the almost relentless stimulation of Jackson Heights, my kitchen becomes my refuge. Whether I'm slicing carrots for a sauce Bolognese or bok choy for a stir-fry, I always find myself drifting into a Buddha-like serenity, a welcome counterpoint to the hubbub beyond my haven.

There must be other women out there who share this experience and could become my friends and guides to their own culinary traditions. I fantasize about posting flyers around the neighborhood: "Help Wanted: Excellent cook from any nation in the world except Europe willing to take on Italian American apprentice. Willing to exchange recipes."

Decades ago when the city was bankrupt and I was unemployed and discouraged, cooking saved my life. What began as a distraction became an act of self-affirmation. Of course I wanted to get out of bed every morning! I was no longer a girl-woman still out of work but a good cook on her way to becoming a much better cook, maybe even a great cook. I was Mother Courage feeding my friends and family, and I had a mission. There were so many new recipes to try and I had all the time I needed. The blanket of worry that used to weigh me down every morning became light as spun sugar or the zabaglione I learned how to whip to celestial heights.

And then my elderly next-door-neighbor, whose name I hadn't even known, took me under her wing. I'd been working my way east through Europe in my international cookbook, pounding and stirring my way out of despondency, and had reached Poland. Meeting one day in our apartment building lobby, she asked me the source of the aromas wafting from my apartment. When I answered, "Mushroom piroshki," my first Polish dish, the lines of her face lifted.

Introducing herself, Margaret made an impression as if I were seeing her for the first time—a woman with gray hair wispy as smoke, deep-set brown eyes and a plump, kindly face. She revealed that she was from Warsaw—later she told me she had miraculously escaped the war in a perilous flight to America. But now we talked about food and cooking. "Would you like some of my recipes?" she asked, almost shyly. Touched by her generosity, I accepted right away. Over the next month, I was treated to hands-on cooking demonstrations as Margaret showed me the proper techniques for achieving sublimely light dough. She became my personal Julia Child—but unlike that popular TV chef, Margaret would pull back two kitchen chairs after our "how-to" sessions. We sat, we savored, we talked.

I remember this experience as I stop into the community center that is Starbucks. We all seem to be refugees rubbing shoulders wherever food is found. The young woman who hands me my latté is pink-cheeked and blue-eyed; a wisp of blond hair escapes from her very unlikely hijab. I can't help wondering if she left her life on an Amish farm for a new Muslim life here. We are all talking in our own languages or a combination—Spanglish, Chinglish—in small groups or plugged in, chatting to invisible friends, Skyping across time zones, or tapping on laptops and smartphones, the teens so cool-looking, peering into their sleek, white iMacs, the older customers reading *The New York Times* or ethnic tabloids that bring the latest homeland news. We are all here together, coexisting harmoniously in our side-by-side universes, our self-made cocoons.

Cafés and bustling restaurants and the vibrant, swarming streets will always draw me because I have an oasis, the block-long park behind our co-op that beckons as I gaze from my sunroom windows. In all seasons but winter, I retreat to its soothing stillness and enter the book of poetry on my lap, pen and pad ready for inspiration. And I enter the language of birds, each word a note in a concert—just as the street sounds, when I'm in that other world, can seem a kind of symphony, the el roaring and receding like a kettle drum.

Eventually, I answer the streets' call and I'm back in the churning of 37th Avenue, turning the corner past the pizzeria, bakery and Columbian restaurant. All kinds of people are stopping for an espresso, a café con leche, a mango lassi, or picking up churros or maybe an empanada for lunch later. I see the Buddhist monks in their orange robes and sandals walking single file. They stop in front of an apartment building where a devout woman places food into their alms bowls.

Nothing has changed throughout history: the rituals and customs of food still define us, and archaeologists still search for meaning in pottery shards, iron pots, and the bones of animals found near charred, fossilized wood. My mind returns to that photo exhibit at the Met on multi-ethnic religious practices in New York, and I recall another image: platters heaped with food that a Vietnamese family had placed before the photo of a loved one on his death anniversary. In ancient Rome, my ancestors visited the cemetery, sharing wine among themselves and funneling some into their relative's grave. Today, observant Chinese do the same, offering food to the deceased, graveside, during Ghost Festivals.

Alive or dead, we need our sustenance. So on the streets of Jackson Heights this 21st century morning, we're converging at an elemental place where we'll gather what's needed to feed ourselves and our families—the "fruited plain" of our Korean greengrocer, where the purple mountains of plums are so high, our hands must climb to reach the top. It's a plain that knows no fence, pushing out to the sidewalk where we sniff, squeeze, exclaim to companions in Farsi, French, English, Urdu, Spanish, Cantonese, Korean, Russian, and Creole.

I take my place in line with the Irish supers, women who peer from burkas, retirees, Croatian carpenters, and turbaned Sikhs with flag pins on their suits—Proud to Be American from sea to shining sea of blueberries, kiwi, yams, yucca, mangoes, guavas, pumpkins. At 10 p.m., Aztec-faced men who built these pyramid displays will sweep up remains, vanishing into a back room with plastic buckets of unsold bouquets. At 8 am tomorrow, Kim and her brother Sam will raise the steel gate once more: This is America. No one starves.

ACKNOWLEDGMENTS

I thank the editors of the following magazines that published these essays, sometimes with slightly different wording.

The Common, "The Cloak Room," "The Spanish Shawl," "The Chemical Company," "A Pilgrimage to 5 Pointz"

The Evansville Review, "Under the River and into the Woods"

Green Mountains Review, "Mystery, Menace and Early Sorrow," "Searching for George, Dan and Fergus," "My Brother's Guns"

Kestrel, "A Facebook Page in Iran"

Literal Latté, "Sicily: My Enigma"

Litro, "Beauty, Truth and Gloves"

Potomac Review, "Beggars," "At Home in the New World"

Thread, "The Last Car"

Tusculum Review, "My Lost Kingdom"

VIA, "Life Inside My Name"

Witness, "Land of the Wounded: A Girl in the V.A."

"Food for Survival" was presented at the John D. Calandra Italian American Institute conference, "The 3 F's in Italian Culture: Critical Approaches to Food, Fashion and Film."

I am especially grateful to Anthony Tamburri, co-founder of Bordighera Press with Fred Gardaphé and Paolo Giordano, for his support of my writing through the publication of my poetry collection *Eye to Eye*, and this debut book of creative nonfiction.

I also thank the editors of the following magazines that published poems featured in these essays, sometimes with slightly different wording.

"The Shoot" was first published in *Heliotrope* magazine.

"Pastorale" appears in *Eye to Eye* (Bordighera Press, 2014).

"In the Land of Emperors" was first published in *Dogwood* and appears in *A Secret Room in Fall* (Ashland Poetry Press, 2006).

ABOUT THE AUTHOR

MARIA TERRONE's creative nonfiction has appeared in such publications as *Witness, Green Mountains Review, The Common, Briar Cliff Review, Potomac Review, The Evansville Review* and *Litro* (U.K.). The title essay of this book, *At Home in the New World*, was based on her piece commissioned by the Guggenheim Museum and performed in several Jackson Heights, Queens, locations for its *stillspotting nyc* project.

As a poet, Terrone is the author of the collections *Eye to Eye* (Bordighera Press); *A Secret Room in Fall* (McGovern Prize, Ashland Poetry Press); *The Bodies We Were Loaned* (The Word Works), and a chapbook, *American Gothic, Take 2* (Finishing Line Press). Magazines including *Poetry, Ploughshares* and *The Hudson Review* and more than 25 anthologies have featured her work, which has been nominated four times for a Pushcart Prize and published in French and Farsi. In 2015 she became the poetry editor of the journal *Italian Americana*.

A native New Yorker, she works as a communications consultant for higher education and lives in Queens with her husband, Bill. Visit her at www.mariaterrone.com

VIA Folios

A refereed book series dedicated to the culture of Italians and Italian Americans.

GIL FAGIANI. *Missing Madonnas*. Vol. 131. Poetry. $14

LEWIS TURCO. *The Sonnetarium*. Vol. 130. Poetry. $12

JOE AMATO. *Samuel Taylor's Hollywood Adventure*. Vol. 129. Novel. $20

BEA TUSIANI. *Con Amore*. Vol. 128. Memoir. $16

MARIA GIURA. *What My Father Taught Me*. Vol. 127. Poetry. $12

STANISLAO PUGLIESE. *A Century of Sinatra*. Vol. 126. Criticism. $12

TONY ARDIZZONE. *The Arab's Ox*. Vol. 125. Novel. $18

PHYLLIS CAPELLO. *Packs Small Plays Big*. Vol. 124. Literature. $10

FRED GARDAPHÉ. *Read 'em and Reap*. Vol. 123. Criticism. $22

JOSEPH A. AMATO. *Diagnostics*. Vol 122. Literature. $12

DENNIS BARONE. *Second Thoughts*. Vol 121. Poetry. $10

OLIVIA K. CERRONE. *The Hunger Saint*. Vol 120. Novella. $12

GARIBLADI M. LAPOLLA. *Miss Rollins in Love*. Vol 119. Novel. $24

JOSEPH TUSIANI. *A Clarion Call*. Vol 118. Poetry. $16

JOSEPH A. AMATO. *My Three Sicilies*. Vol 117. Poetry & Prose. $17

MARGHERITA COSTA. *Voice of a Virtuosa and Coutesan*. Vol 116. Poetry. $24

NICOLE SANTALUCIA. *Because I Did Not Die*. Vol 115. Poetry. $12

MARK CIABATTARI. *Preludes to History*. Vol 114. Poetry. $12

HELEN BAROLINI. *Visits*. Vol 113. Novel. $22

ERNESTO LIVORNI. *The Fathers' America*. Vol 112. Poetry. $14

MARIO B. MIGNONE. *The Story of My People*. Vol 111. Non-fiction. $17

GEORGE GUIDA. *The Sleeping Gulf*. Vol 110. Poetry. $14

JOEY NICOLETTI. *Reverse Graffiti*. Vol 109. Poetry. $14

GIOSE RIMANELLI. *Il mestiere del furbo*. Vol 108. Criticism. $20

LEWIS TURCO. *The Hero Enkidu*. Vol 107. Poetry. $14

AL TACCONELLI. *Perhaps Fly*. Vol 106. Poetry. $14

RACHEL GUIDO DEVRIES. *A Woman Unknown in Her Bones*. Vol 105. Poetry. $11

BERNARD BRUNO. *A Tear and a Tear in My Heart*. Vol 104. Non-fiction. $20

FELIX STEFANILE. *Songs of the Sparrow*. Vol 103. Poetry. $30

FRANK POLIZZI. *A New Life with Bianca*. Vol 102. Poetry. $10

GIL FAGIANI. *Stone Walls*. Vol 101. Poetry. $14

LOUISE DESALVO. *Casting Off*. Vol 100. Fiction. $22

MARY JO BONA. *I Stop Waiting for You*. Vol 99. Poetry. $12

RACHEL GUIDO DEVRIES. *Stati zitt, Josie*. Vol 98. Children's Literature. $8

GRACE CAVALIERI. *The Mandate of Heaven*. Vol 97. Poetry. $14

MARISA FRASCA. *Via incanto*. Vol 96. Poetry. $12

DOUGLAS GLADSTONE. *Carving a Niche for Himself*. Vol 95. History. $12

MARIA TERRONE. *Eye to Eye*. Vol 94. Poetry. $14

CONSTANCE SANCETTA. *Here in Cerchio*. Vol 93. Local History. $15

MARIA MAZZIOTTI GILLAN. *Ancestors' Song*. Vol 92. Poetry. $14

MICHAEL PARENTI. *Waiting for Yesterday: Pages from a Street Kid's Life*. Vol 90. Memoir. $15

ANNIE LANZILLOTTO. *Schistsong*. Vol 89. Poetry. $15

EMANUEL DI PASQUALE. *Love Lines*. Vol 88. Poetry. $10

CAROSONE & LOGIUDICE. *Our Naked Lives*. Vol 87. Essays. $15

JAMES PERICONI. *Strangers in a Strange Land: A Survey of Italian-Language American Books*.Vol 86. Book History. $24

DANIELA GIOSEFFI. *Escaping La Vita Della Cucina*. Vol 85. Essays. $22

MARIA FAMÀ. *Mystics in the Family*. Vol 84. Poetry. $10

ROSSANA DEL ZIO. *From Bread and Tomatoes to Zuppa di Pesce "Ciambotto"*.Vol. 83. $15

LORENZO DELBOCA. *Polentoni*. Vol 82. Italian Studies. $15

SAMUEL GHELLI. *A Reference Grammar*. Vol 81. Italian Language. $36

ROSS TALARICO. *Sled Run*. Vol 80. Fiction. $15

FRED MISURELLA. *Only Sons*. Vol 79. Fiction. $14

FRANK LENTRICCHIA. *The Portable Lentricchia*. Vol 78. Fiction. $16

RICHARD VETERE. *The Other Colors in a Snow Storm*. Vol 77. Poetry. $10

GARIBALDI LAPOLLA. *Fire in the Flesh*. Vol 76 Fiction & Criticism. $25

GEORGE GUIDA. *The Pope Stories*. Vol 75 Prose. $15

ROBERT VISCUSI. *Ellis Island*. Vol 74. Poetry. $28

ELENA GIANINI BELOTTI. *The Bitter Taste of Strangers Bread*. Vol 73. Fiction. $24

PINO APRILE. *Terroni*. Vol 72. Italian Studies. $20

EMANUEL DI PASQUALE. *Harvest*. Vol 71. Poetry. $10

ROBERT ZWEIG. *Return to Naples*. Vol 70. Memoir. $16

AIROS & CAPPELLI. *Guido*. Vol 69. Italian/American Studies. $12

FRED GARDAPHÉ. *Moustache Pete is Dead! Long Live Moustache Pete!*. Vol 67. Literature/Oral History. $12

PAOLO RUFFILLI. *Dark Room/Camera oscura*. Vol 66. Poetry. $11

HELEN BAROLINI. *Crossing the Alps*. Vol 65. Fiction. $14

COSMO FERRARA. *Profiles of Italian Americans*. Vol 64. Italian Americana. $16

GIL FAGIANI. *Chianti in Connecticut*. Vol 63. Poetry. $10

BASSETTI & D'ACQUINO. *Italic Lessons*. Vol 62. Italian/American Studies. $10

CAVALIERI & PASCARELLI, Eds. *The Poet's Cookbook*. Vol 61. Poetry/Recipes. $12

EMANUEL DI PASQUALE. *Siciliana*. Vol 60. Poetry. $8

NATALIA COSTA, Ed. *Bufalini*. Vol 59. Poetry. $18.

RICHARD VETERE. *Baroque*. Vol 58. Fiction. $18.

LEWIS TURCO. *La Famiglia/The Family*. Vol 57. Memoir. $15

NICK JAMES MILETI. *The Unscrupulous*. Vol 56. Humanities. $20

BASSETTI. ACCOLLA. D'AQUINO. *Italici: An Encounter with Piero Bassetti.* Vol 55. Italian Studies. $8

GIOSE RIMANELLI. *The Three-legged One.* Vol 54. Fiction. $15

CHARLES KLOPP. *Bele Antiche Stòrie.* Vol 53. Criticism. $25

JOSEPH RICAPITO. *Second Wave.* Vol 52. Poetry. $12

GARY MORMINO. *Italians in Florida.* Vol 51. History. $15

GIANFRANCO ANGELUCCI. *Federico F.* Vol 50. Fiction. $15

ANTHONY VALERIO. *The Little Sailor.* Vol 49. Memoir. $9

ROSS TALARICO. *The Reptilian Interludes.* Vol 48. Poetry. $15

RACHEL GUIDO DE VRIES. *Teeny Tiny Tino's Fishing Story.* Vol 47. Children's Literature. $6

EMANUEL DI PASQUALE. *Writing Anew.* Vol 46. Poetry. $15

MARIA FAMÀ. *Looking For Cover.* Vol 45. Poetry. $12

ANTHONY VALERIO. *Toni Cade Bambara's One Sicilian Night.* Vol 44. Poetry. $10

EMANUEL CARNEVALI. *Furnished Rooms.* Vol 43. Poetry. $14

BRENT ADKINS. et al., Ed. *Shifting Borders. Negotiating Places.* Vol 42. Conference. $18

GEORGE GUIDA. *Low Italian.* Vol 41. Poetry. $11

GARDAPHÈ, GIORDANO, TAMBURRI. *Introducing Italian Americana.* Vol 40. Italian/American Studies. $10

DANIELA GIOSEFFI. *Blood Autumn/Autunno di sangue.* Vol 39. Poetry. $15/$25

FRED MISURELLA. *Lies to Live By.* Vol 38. Stories. $15

STEVEN BELLUSCIO. *Constructing a Bibliography.* Vol 37. Italian Americana. $15

ANTHONY JULIAN TAMBURRI, Ed. *Italian Cultural Studies 2002.* Vol 36. Essays. $18

BEA TUSIANI. *con amore.* Vol 35. Memoir. $19

FLAVIA BRIZIO-SKOV, Ed. *Reconstructing Societies in the Aftermath of War.* Vol 34. History. $30

TAMBURRI. et al., Eds. *Italian Cultural Studies 2001.* Vol 33. Essays. $18

ELIZABETH G. MESSINA, Ed. *In Our Own Voices.* Vol 32. Italian/American Studies. $25

STANISLAO G. PUGLIESE. *Desperate Inscriptions.* Vol 31. History. $12

HOSTERT & TAMBURRI, Eds. *Screening Ethnicity.* Vol 30. Italian/American Culture. $25

G. PARATI & B. LAWTON, Eds. *Italian Cultural Studies.* Vol 29. Essays. $18

HELEN BAROLINI. *More Italian Hours.* Vol 28. Fiction. $16

FRANCO NASI, Ed. *Intorno alla Via Emilia.* Vol 27. Culture. $16

ARTHUR L. CLEMENTS. *The Book of Madness & Love.* Vol 26. Poetry. $10

JOHN CASEY, et al. *Imagining Humanity.* Vol 25. Interdisciplinary Studies. $18

ROBERT LIMA. *Sardinia/Sardegna.* Vol 24. Poetry. $10

DANIELA GIOSEFFI. *Going On.* Vol 23. Poetry. $10

ROSS TALARICO. *The Journey Home*. Vol 22. Poetry. $12

EMANUEL DI PASQUALE. *The Silver Lake Love Poems*. Vol 21. Poetry. $7

JOSEPH TUSIANI. *Ethnicity*. Vol 20. Poetry. $12

JENNIFER LAGIER. *Second Class Citizen*. Vol 19. Poetry. $8

FELIX STEFANILE. *The Country of Absence*. Vol 18. Poetry. $9

PHILIP CANNISTRARO. *Blackshirts*. Vol 17. History. $12

LUIGI RUSTICHELLI, Ed. *Seminario sul racconto*. Vol 16. Narrative. $10

LEWIS TURCO. *Shaking the Family Tree*. Vol 15. Memoirs. $9

LUIGI RUSTICHELLI, Ed. *Seminario sulla drammaturgia*. Vol 14. Theater/ Essays. $10

FRED GARDAPHÈ. *Moustache Pete is Dead! Long Live Moustache Pete!*. Vol 13. Oral Literature. $10

JONE GAILLARD CORSI. *Il libretto d'autore. 1860–1930*. Vol 12. Criticism. $17

HELEN BAROLINI. *Chiaroscuro: Essays of Identity*. Vol 11. Essays. $15

PICARAZZI & FEINSTEIN, Eds. *An African Harlequin in Milan*. Vol 10. Theater/Essays. $15

JOSEPH RICAPITO. *Florentine Streets & Other Poems*. Vol 9. Poetry. $9

FRED MISURELLA. *Short Time*. Vol 8. Novella. $7

NED CONDINI. *Quartettsatz*. Vol 7. Poetry. $7

ANTHONY JULIAN TAMBURRI, Ed. *Fuori: Essays by Italian/American Lesbiansand Gays*. Vol 6. Essays. $10

ANTONIO GRAMSCI. P. Verdicchio. Trans. & Intro. *The Southern Question*. Vol 5.Social Criticism. $5

DANIELA GIOSEFFI. *Word Wounds & Water Flowers*. Vol 4. Poetry. $8

WILEY FEINSTEIN. *Humility's Deceit: Calvino Reading Ariosto Reading Calvino*. Vol 3. Criticism. $10

PAOLO A. GIORDANO, Ed. *Joseph Tusiani: Poet. Translator. Humanist*. Vol 2. Criticism. $25

ROBERT VISCUSI. *Oration Upon the Most Recent Death of Christopher Columbus*. Vol 1. Poetry.

CPSIA information can be obtained
at www.ICGtesting.com
Printed in the USA
FSHW01n0245110718
50082FS

9 781599 541273